CHILD
THE NEW FOREST

CAPTAIN MARRYAT R.N.

Simplified by Michael West

Illustrated by Geoffrey Whittan

1,200 word vocabulary

LONGMAN

LONGMAN GROUP LIMITED
Longman House,
Burnt Mill, Harlow, Essex, U.K.

First published in this edition 1937
Second edition (reset and re-illustrated, twenty-fourth printing) 1962
New impressions *1963; *1964 (thrice);
1966; *1967; *1968 (twice);
*1969; *1970; *1971;
*1973; *1974;
*1976; *1977;
*1978; *1980;
*1981

ISBN 0 582 53450 X

We are grateful to the BBC for permission to reproduce the photograph on the cover. We also thank Richard Gibson, Timandra Alwin, Edwina Ashton and Arthur Campbell who appear as the Children of the New Forest in the photograph.

Printed in Hong Kong by
Dai Nippon Printing Co (H.K.) Ltd

Illustrations

Contents

One

THE KING ESCAPES

Nearly three hundred years ago, the people of England rose and fought against their king, Charles the First. In the end they won a great battle at Naseby, made him a prisoner, and formed a new government.

Among the friends of King Charles who died fighting bravely at Naseby was a certain *Colonel*[1] Beverley. His home was at Arnwood, in the New Forest, in the South of England. When poor Mrs. Beverley heard that her husband was dead, she became so sad and ill that she also died very soon after him. Colonel Beverley and his wife had four children, Edward, Humphrey, Alice and Edith. Edward was fourteen years of age, Humphrey twelve, Alice eleven, and Edith eight.

England was then not a happy place for the friends of the King who had fought on his side. Their lands and houses and riches were taken from them. Many of them left their homes and went over the sea to other countries. Thus when their mother died, the four children were left without anyone to take care of them, except an old servant, Jacob Armitage. Most of Colonel Beverley's other

---

[1] Colonel = A man who commands about a thousand men in the army.

servants had followed him to fight for the King; some were killed at Naseby, the others were prisoners.

Jacob lived in a little house about a mile and a half from Arnwood. When his master went to join the King's army, he asked the old man to go and live at the great house and guard the four children and their mother. But Jacob had lived all his life in the forest, and although he loved his master he felt that he could not leave it in his old age. He promised to go every day to Arnwood and do everything he could to help the children. He kept his promise. Day after day he went to the great house and did whatever was needed to help his master's family. When Mrs. Beverley died, worn out with sadness, Jacob felt that it was his duty to take the place of both father and mother to the four children. Thus they lived at Arnwood when King Charles escaped from his prison near London.

As soon as the escape of the King became known, bands of horse-soldiers were sent to follow him and bring him back to prison. It was soon known that the King had gone towards the New Forest. His enemies thought that he meant to sail across the sea from some town on the South Coast, and that he would first hide in the forest until a ship was ready for him. Small bands of horsemen therefore rode through the forest, to try to stop him before he reached the coast.

It was evening. Jacob was returning to his own house in the forest. Then he saw some soldiers riding between the trees. He knew by their clothes that they were the King's enemies, and that he was in danger. Very quietly he stood behind a thick tree and watched them get down from their horses in order to give them a rest. One man, the captain, stood with his hand upon his horse's neck. "Is there any man here who knows the forest well?" he asked. "We cannot stay here long, and we have a great deal of work to do."

"Yes, sir," replied another man. "I am James Southwold. I was born in the forest, and have worked here all my life."

Jacob looked at the man who had just spoken, and remembered his face. He was one of the men from a village near Arnwood who had joined the King's army when the war started. Jacob had thought that James Southwold was an honourable, true-hearted young man, and he was surprised and sad to find that he had now joined the King's enemies.

"If you were born in the forest, you must know all its paths," said the leader. "Are there any secret places in it where a man can be hidden?"

"I know one place, between two low hills, where a band of soldiers with their horses could be hidden from everybody's eyes," replied Southwold. "It is near Arnwood."

"We will ride there, then," replied the captain. "Is not Arnwood the house of Beverley, who was killed at Naseby?"

"Yes, and I have eaten many good meals there,"

said Southwold. "Perhaps the King may be hidden there."

"Well, we will ride first to this place between the hills," replied the captain. "If we do not find him there, we will go on to Arnwood at night. These old houses are full of secret rooms and passages, but fire will drive forth any man who may be hiding in them. To horse!"

The soldiers sprang to their horses, and rode through the trees; Southwold showed them the way. Jacob stood behind the tree until they were out of sight. "And so the King has escaped," he thought. "He may be at Arnwood. Even if he is not there, the children will be in danger. These soldiers will set fire to the house, and the children will be burnt to death. I must hurry to the house and help them to escape." In less than an hour he had returned to Arnwood.

Two

FIRE AT ARNWOOD

Miss Judith Villiers was sitting in the great hall at Arnwood. A servant came in. "Old Jacob wishes to see you," he said.

Mrs. Beverley, mother of the four children, of whom we spoke in the first chapter, was dead.

Just before her death she asked her sister, Miss Judith Villiers, to come to Arnwood, to take care of the house, and rule the few servants who remained.

Old Jacob was one of the old servants and he did most of the work.

"What is it, Jacob?" asked Miss Villiers.

"I must first tell you that King Charles has escaped from prison. People think that he is hidden in the forest near Arnwood, or even in the house itself. Only an hour ago I saw a party of soldiers riding through the forest-paths. I heard them talking, and discovered that they were coming here to seek for the King. They said that they would set fire to the house even if they did not find him."

"And what do you wish me to do?" asked Miss Judith.

"My lady, I think that you and the children should leave Arnwood and come to my little house in the forest. It is only a poor place, and is not fit for you, but you will be in great danger if you remain here."

"No, Jacob. No enemy of King Charles can make me afraid, or drive me out of my own home. Whatever happens, I shall remain."

"But, my lady, the children cannot stay. I will not leave them here. I promised my master——"

"Will the children be in greater danger than I?" replied the lady angrily. "These soldiers will treat me as a lady should be treated. They will never dare to hurt me."

"I am afraid that they will dare to do anything they wish, my lady. The children will be afraid of them. For one night at least they will be safer if they come with me," replied Jacob.

"Well then; take them to your house."

Jacob knew that the proud Miss Judith would never give way to his wishes, nor leave the house in fear of the soldiers. He therefore went to look for the children. He found them playing in the garden. He called the two boys to him and told them to follow him. "Now, Edward," he said, "your father was a brave man. The time has come when you must be as brave as he was. We must leave this house at once."

"But why, Jacob? Tell me why," answered Edward.

"Because the soldiers will burn it down to-night," said Jacob.

"Burn it down! The house is mine. Who dares to burn down this house?"

"They will dare, and they will do it, too."

"But we will fight them, Jacob."

"And what can you and I do against twenty horsemen?" asked Jacob with a smile. "Remember your sisters. Do you wish to see them shot or burnt to death? No, Edward, you must do as I say. You must all come with me to the little house in the forest. Get whatever clothes you need, load them onto the horse, and come at once."

"That will be fine," cried Humphrey. But

Edward would not at first give way. Now that his father was dead, he felt that he was the head of the family. He wished to stay and guard Arnwood against the King's enemies, but at last Jacob made him understand that the danger to his little sisters was too great. Hurriedly they gathered together the things that they needed. They were almost ready to go, and were calling the little girls to go with them, when Edward asked suddenly, "Is Aunt[1] Judith coming with us?"

"She will not leave the house," replied Jacob; "she means to stay and speak to the soldiers."

"And so an old woman remains to guard the house, while I run away!" said Edward. "No! I will not go."

"Well, do as you wish," replied Jacob. "But we cannot leave your sisters here. They and Humphrey must come with me, and I cannot bring them if you do not help me. Come with us. The house is not far away, and you can return in a very short time."

"Yes, I will do that," replied Edward.

The horse was soon loaded, and the little girls, who were still playing in the garden, were called in by Humphrey. They were told that they were going to Jacob's house for the night, and they were delighted.

"Now, Edward," said Jacob, "will you take your sisters by the hand and lead them to my house? Here is the key of the door; Humphrey

[1] Aunt = The sister of a father or mother; the wife of an uncle.

can lead the horse." He then took Edward aside. "I must tell you one thing that I do not wish your brother and sisters to know. King Charles has escaped. The New Forest is full of soldiers looking for him, and so you must not leave them until I return. Shut the house-door with the iron bar as soon as it is dark. You will find a lamp in the kitchen; my gun is loaded, and is hanging over the fire-place. If the soldiers try to come in, you must do your best to keep them out. But you must promise me not to leave the house until I come back. I shall stay here to see what happens. When I come back, we can decide upon the best plan."

Edward promised that he would not leave his sisters. Just before darkness fell, the little party passed through the gateway of Arnwood. Jacob returned to the great hall, where Miss Judith was still sitting.

"I wish, my lady," he said, "that you would leave this house. I am sure it is dangerous to stay here."

"Jacob Armitage, I would not leave this house, even if it were filled with soldiers. Leave me, and never return. Do as I order. Send my servant-girl to me."

"My lady, I have just seen all the servants leaving the house. When I go, you will be alone."

"Have they dared to leave?" shouted the lady.

"My lady, they dared not stay," said Jacob.

"Then leave me too," answered the proud old lady. "And shut the door when you go out."

When Jacob found that he could not get Miss Judith to leave the house, he went out as he was ordered, and followed the children along the road.

About a mile away from Arnwood there was a small *inn* at the side of the road. When Jacob came near, he found it filled with the soldiers whom he had seen in the forest. Their horses were tied to the trees outside the inn, while the soldiers drank inside. Jacob entered, with the thought that he might find out whether the soldiers really meant to set fire to Arnwood. James Southwold was sitting at a table. As soon as he saw Jacob, whom he had known for many years, he asked many questions about the family at Arnwood. Jacob answered him, and then suddenly thought of a plan to save Miss Judith.

"You are going to Arnwood," he said, "and I have heard what you are looking for. Well, if you meet an old lady, or something that looks like an old lady, take her on your horse and ride away as fast as you can. I dare not say any more, but I am sure you understand."

"Yes," replied Southwold in a low voice. "The lady is not a lady, but——" He had no time to finish his words, for the order was given to get on their horses, and the soldiers rode away. Jacob followed them unseen. They soon arrived at the great house, got off their horses, and entered. From where Jacob was standing, a little distance away, he could see lights moving from room to room. In a few minutes fire broke out from the lower windows, and soon the whole house was burning.

Jacob turned to go back to his house, when he heard the sound of a horse's feet, and a loud cry of anger. A minute afterwards James Southwold passed him; behind him was tied Miss Judith; she was kicking and fighting to get free. Jacob smiled. He knew that his little plan had saved Miss Judith's life, for it was plain that Southwold thought that his prisoner was King Charles dressed as an old lady. In half an hour Jacob reached his house. By this time the fire at Arnwood was throwing its light all round the country. Jacob stood at the door and called softly. Edward opened it.

"Come out, Edward," said Jacob, "and look." Edward saw the great fire lighting the sky. He was silent.

"I told you that this would happen," Jacob said. "You would all have been burnt in your beds. The soldiers did not look to see who was in the house; they set fire to it as soon as they reached it."

"But what has happened to my aunt?" cried Edward.

"She is quite safe. By this time she must be far away from the fire," replied Jacob. "But we are still in danger. The King's enemies must not discover that the children of Colonel Beverley have escaped. I shall go into Lymington to-morrow. The soldiers are staying there, and I must find out what they mean to do, and what has happened to Miss Judith. You must remain here, and take care of your sisters until I return. Look, the fire is not so bright as it was."

"No," replied Edward. "But it is my house that is destroyed."

"It was your house, Edward, but I am afraid that the new government will take it away from you, with all the lands around it. They have done this with the lands of other officers who fought for the King. But come in; it is very late, and the night is cold."

Edward slowly followed Jacob into the house. His heart was full of anger. These men had killed his father. They had burnt his house and stolen his land. He lay down on the bed. For a long time he could not sleep. Wild plans passed through his mind; but at last he slept. Strange dreams came to him, and he often called loudly in his sleep, and woke his brothers and sisters.

Three

THE CHILDREN IN THE FOREST

The next morning Jacob gave the children their breakfast; then he set off towards Arnwood. The house was almost completely destroyed by the fire. A few men and women stood near, drawn there by curiosity. Among them Jacob noticed Benjamin, one of the servants who had left the house the day before. He went up to him and said, "Well, Benjamin, this is a sad sight. Do you know what has happened at Lymington?"

"Lymington is full of soldiers," replied Benjamin, "and their manners are not very good."

"And where is the old lady?" asked Jacob.

"Ah, that's a sad business," replied Benjamin. "James Southwold thought that she was King Charles dressed as an old woman. So he carried her away on his horse, but she kicked and fought so hard that they both fell off and broke their necks."

"Then the old lady is dead?" asked Jacob.

"Yes, she is," replied Benjamin. "Poor children! I was at the inn, and the soldiers were laughing at the work they had done. I was very angry. I asked one of them whether it was a good thing to burn children in their beds. 'Of course it is,' he replied. 'If you kill a fox, and find its young ones, don't you kill them too?' I didn't say another word, but came out. I might have got into trouble."

"Have you heard anything about the King?" asked Jacob.

"No, but the soldiers still think he is in the forest. Bands of horsemen are riding through it to try and discover his hiding-place."

Benjamin's words filled Jacob with doubt and fear. He said "Good-bye" to Benjamin, and hurried back to the house. "Well," he thought,

"I'm sorry for the old lady, but I must think of the children now. Kill the little foxes! Yes, but they must find them first!"

Jacob found the children outside the door, waiting for him. They ran up to him, and asked a thousand questions about their home and the fire which had destroyed it. But Jacob made them go inside. "The soldiers are riding all through the forest," he said, "and they must not see you here."

"Will they harm this house too?" asked little Alice, as she took Jacob's hand.

"Yes, I think they would, if they found you here; but we must not let them see you."

They all entered the house. There was one large room in front, and three small bedrooms behind.

"Now, what can we have for dinner? There's some meat left, I know. We must all help. Who will be cook?"

"I will be cook," said Alice, "if you will show me how to cook."

"Yes, Alice," answered Jacob, "you shall be cook."

The dinner was soon ready.

"Now, you see you have cooked your own dinner. Isn't that pleasant?" said Jacob.

"Yes," they all cried; "and we will eat it too, as soon as it is on the table!" Humphrey and Alice laid the table, Edith found the salt, Edward stood on guard at the door, watching the forest for signs of the soldiers. While the dinner was being cooked,

Jacob showed the children how to put everything in order in the room. They worked happily together, until Edward came in and said, "Here are some soldiers riding towards the house!"

Jacob called the children together, and said, "These men may come and look into every room in the house. You must do as I tell you. You must be very quiet. Humphrey, you and your sisters must go to bed, and pretend to be very ill. Edward, take off your coat, and put on this old coat of mine. You must stay in the bedroom and attend to your sick brother and sisters. Come, Edith, you must play at going to bed, and have your dinner later."

The children quietly did as Jacob told them. Then the soldiers appeared at the door.

"Come in," said Jacob to their leader.

"Who are you, my friend?" asked he.

"A poor *forester*, in great trouble," answered Jacob.

"What is your trouble, my man?"

"All my children are very sick. If you make too much noise, they will not get better."

"But we must look into every room," the leader said.

"You may do so," said Jacob, "but try to be very quiet." He opened the doors of all the rooms, and the soldiers passed through. Little Edith cried with fear when she saw them; but Edward kissed her, and told her to be brave. The soldiers took no notice of the children, but came back to the front room.

"Well, there's no one hidden here," said one of the soldiers. "Shall we go? I'm very tired and hungry with our long ride."

"So am I," said another. "Something here smells very good." He took the cover off the pot. "What's this, my man?"

"My dinner for a week," replied Jacob. "I have no one to cook for me now, and I can't light a fire every day."

"You seem to have very good food here. I should like to taste it."

"I will gladly give you some, and cook some more for myself," replied Jacob.

The soldiers sat down at the table, and very soon the children's dinner had gone. When the men had finished their meal, they told Jacob that they had enjoyed it very much. Then with a laugh, they got on their horses and rode away.

As soon as they were out of sight Jacob called to the children to get up again. They came running out of the bedroom, hungry for their dinners.

"They've gone now," said Jacob.

"And our dinners have gone too," said Humphrey, looking at the empty pot. But soon many hands were at work. They prepared a second dinner, which they enjoyed all the more for having had to wait so long for it.

"This is very fine," said Humphrey, with his mouth full.

"Yes," replied Jacob; "I doubt whether King Charles is eating so good a dinner to-day. Edward, you seem very silent and serious!"

"Yes, I am," said Edward. "I have reason to be serious. I wish I could have fought those soldiers!"

"But you could not; no doubt your chance will come. Who knows? King Charles may soon return at the head of an army," replied Jacob.

They had no more visitors to the house that day. The next morning, Jacob told Edward what to do if the soldiers returned. He then rode to the inn to find out what had happened after the fire at Arnwood. There he learnt that King Charles had been taken prisoner again. He had been sent to the Isle of Wight, an island near the South Coast of England. The soldiers who had been looking for him in the forest were returning to London. Jacob then rode into Lymington, bought some clothes for the children, and then returned home.

When he arrived at the little house, he said, "You must now wear such clothes as poor people in the forest wear. Your fine silk dresses will soon be worn out if you wander through the forest paths. Edward and Humphrey too will need stronger clothes for the work they will do. Now remember," he went on; "if anybody asks who you are, you must say you are my grandchildren. No one must know that you are the children of Colonel Beverley. Edward understands why this must be so, and some day you will all understand."

The children soon changed their clothes and ran out of the cottage to play, delighted with their freedom.

Four

EDWARD'S FIRST LESSON

That night, Jacob lay awake for a long time. He wondered what was the best way to guard the children against the dangers in which they were placed. What would happen to them if he died? He was an old man. He could not live very long. "I must teach them to be useful," he thought, "and they must begin to-morrow the life of forest children."

The next morning, as soon as the children were ready for breakfast, he called them into the sitting-room and said, "My dear children, you must remain here, so that the soldiers may not discover you; they killed your father. If I had not taken you away, they would have burnt you in your beds. You must live here as my grandchildren, and take the name of Armitage instead of Beverley; you must dress like children of the forest, and do as they do. You must do everything for yourselves, for there are no servants to do the work for you. We must all work; but if we all work together, the work will only be play. Now Edward is the oldest; he must come into the forest with me. I will teach him to kill the *deer* for our food. When he has learnt this lesson, then Humphrey shall come out and learn to shoot."

"Yes," said Humphrey, "I'll soon learn."

"But not yet," replied Jacob. "First you must take care of the horse, and learn to dig in the garden. Alice, dear, you must help Humphrey to light the fire and clean the house every morning. Humphrey will go to the well for water, and you, Alice, must learn to make our clothes, and to cook our meals, and make the beds. Little Edith can take care of the hens and feed them, and look for the eggs every morning—will you, Edith?"

"Yes," answered Edith, "and feed all the little ones, as I did at Arnwood."

"I am sure you will be very useful, my dear. Now, do you all like what I have asked you to do?"

"Yes," they all replied.

After breakfast, when they ate cold meat and plain bread, Jacob took Edward and their dog into the forest to find a deer. Their stock of *venison*[1] was almost finished. This was the first time that Edward had been in the forest to seek for food. He was greatly excited. Jacob smiled, and told him that he must be very careful and quiet. "Remember, you must be hidden, for a deer's eyes are very good. You must be very quiet, because his ears can hear the smallest sound. You must never come up to him the same way as the wind, because his nose can smell a man a mile away. We shall go among those thick trees in front of us; there are some clear spaces there. We must keep to the left hand, for the wind is in the east, and we must walk against it."

[1] Venison = Deer-meat.

One of the deer lifted its head.

They went on for more than a mile. Then Jacob made a sign to Edward, and dropped on his hands and knees. Some distance in front of them four deer were feeding. Edward too went forward on hands and knees, and little by little they got nearer. Then one of the deer lifted its head.

It looked around, and walked away. The others followed, until they were quite half a mile away. Jacob turned to Edward and said, "You see how careful a man must be when he tries to come up to a deer. When you were behind me, you put your foot on a piece of broken stick."

"Yes," replied Edward; "but that made only a little noise."

"It was quite enough to surprise the deer. It made him move away. Now we must walk in a circle to the other side of them."

In half an hour they found the deer again, about three hundred yards away. Jacob and Edward again went on their hands and knees. Slowly and silently they moved from tree to tree. They were two hundred feet away. Carefully Jacob raised his gun to shoot. The tallest deer raised his head; he had heard the sound. He turned his head towards Jacob. Jacob fired and hit the deer. The animal jumped high in the air. He fell to his knees. He tried to rise and run, but fell dead. The other deer ran away as fast as the wind.

Edward jumped to his feet with a shout of joy. He ran forward to the fallen deer. Jacob held him back. "Never do that," he said, "there may be another deer lying down among the long grass. But now your shout has told him that there is danger. We shall never find him."

"Yes, I was wrong," replied Edward; "but I shall know better another time."

They then returned to the house, and brought the horse back to carry the deer home. As soon as they arrived, they sat down to a fine dinner. Alice cooked it. She was very proud of her work when Jacob told her that he had never eaten a better meal.

The next day, Jacob went into Lymington to sell some of the venison. Edward wished to go with him; but Jacob said that if he were seen there, it would be dangerous for them all. He returned in the evening with a long gun for Edward; for Humphrey he bought everything that was needed for work in the garden. Edward at once started to learn how to shoot. In a very short time he showed that he had a very good eye. He could hit a mark at almost every shot a hundred yards away.

"I wish you would let me go out by myself," he cried; "I am sure I could hit and kill a deer."

"No, my boy," replied Jacob. "You have a great deal to learn yet. But I promise that the next time we go out together, you shall have the first shot."

It was now winter, and very cold. The girls remained in the house almost every day. Jacob and the boys went out to get firewood. They brought it home over the snow with ropes. But most of the time was spent in learning to do the work of the house. Alice learnt to work and cook. Sometimes at first she burnt her fingers; she broke the cups and pots, but as the days passed, she became more and more used to the work. Soon she could do her work as well as any cook. Humphrey made several useful little things out of wood, and even Edith learnt how to make little cakes for their breakfast, and helped Alice in her work. It was indeed surprising how much the children could do, now that they had no servants to work for them. In the evening Alice sat and worked with her needle; Jacob taught Alice and Humphrey to read.

Thus the winter passed very quickly. Although they had been living in the forest for five months, the time seemed no longer than five weeks. They were all very happy; but Edward sometimes was sad when he thought of Arnwood. This is not surprising. He lived near the house and lands which should have been his own. He wished he were old enough to fight for the King against those who had burnt down his house and taken his lands. Jacob tried to make him forget his wrongs and forgive his enemies; but Edward thought only of the time when he could take his place as the master of Arnwood, and friend of the King.

Five

BUSY DAYS

The winter passed quickly. The snow no longer lay on the ground. New leaves appeared on the trees. Jacob and Edward could now leave the cottage to find the feeding-places of the deer. At last, to the boy's delight, he shot his first deer and brought it home. Humphrey was beginning to be busy in the garden. He dug the ground and planted the seeds. Edith too was busy, for the hens had begun to lay their eggs again. The grass in the fields grew high and thick. It would soon be ready to be cut and dried as winter food for the horse and the cow.

The summer came; the plants and trees in the garden gave them flowers and fruit and many kinds of food. The children's days were full of happy, busy hours. They hardly noticed how quickly the days passed. One day Jacob told them that it was exactly a year since they had come to live with him. "You are most happy," he said, "when the days pass quickly. You have plenty of work to do. You live here safely and in peace. You are all strong and healthy. People who knew you a year ago could hardly believe that you are the same children!"

The second winter now came. At first Jacob and Edward went out to the forest about twice a week. Soon the old man found that he was unable to follow the deer. Humphrey took his place. Jacob was still strong enough to drive the horse and cart into Lymington. He sold the venison there and bought the things needed for the house. The children saw, however, that even these journeys tired the old man. One day, he wished to cross the forest to bring home two little dogs that a *forest-keeper*[1] had promised to give him. But he felt so weak that he could not rise from his bed. He called Edward, and told him the way to the keeper's house. "You must call yourself Armitage," he said. "Say that you are my grandson. No one must know that you are Edward Beverley."

Edward promised to do as Jacob wished. He set out to ride through the forest. For a short distance Humphrey walked by the horse's side. "I wish I were going with you," he said.

"I wish you were," replied Edward. "I feel like a prisoner set free. Our father was a good soldier. If I were old enough I should escape and join the King's friends. Jacob is kind and good, but I am not fit for this kind of life."

"But remember," said Humphrey, "the old man is getting very old and very weak. What would our sisters do if you left them?"

"I have no thought of leaving them, you may be sure; but I wish we could take them to friends, where they could be safe. Then I should be free to do what I wish."

[1] Forest-keeper = A man who takes care of the wild animals in a forest.

"What would you do if you left the forest?" asked Humphrey.

"I should say who I am, and ask for the lands at Arnwood to be given to me. They are mine, because I am my father's oldest son."

"Yes, that is what Jacob thinks," said Humphrey. "He says that the King's enemies will never let you return to Arnwood. The lands are no longer yours. The King's enemies have taken everything because our father fought for him. They would treat you as an enemy. They would put you in prison, as they have treated the King."

"Why did Jacob not tell me this?" asked Edward.

"He was afraid that you would do something foolishly daring. Your enemies would discover who you were. They would find out that we were hiding in the forest, and our sisters would be sent away. People would find pleasure in treating the daughters of Colonel Beverley badly."

"Humphrey, what you say is true. I am not so foolish as Jacob thinks. I know that I can do nothing while King Charles is a prisoner, and his friends beaten in battle. I am willing to live in the forest and keep quiet; but I must sometimes find out what is happening in the country. The time will come, I am sure, when I shall be able to win back my father's lands and be master of Arnwood."

"I wish that myself," said Humphrey. He turned to go back to his work at the house.

Six

STRANGERS IN THE FOREST

Edward crossed the forest. Just before noon he arrived at the gate of the keeper's house. He passed through a pretty garden. A girl was gathering flowers.

"Is Oswald Partridge at home, please?" asked Edward.

"No, young man, he is in the forest. But I will speak to my father, if you will wait."

In a few minutes the girl returned. She said that her father wished to speak to him. Edward followed her into a room. A man was sitting before a table covered with papers. He was dressed as a "Roundhead", one of the King's enemies, and was reading a letter. He did not look up as Edward entered. This made the boy angry. He forgot that he was supposed to be a poor forester's son, and not Edward Beverley. But then he remembered, and stood silent. At last the man finished reading his letter, and looked at Edward.

"What is your business, young man?" he asked.

"I have come to see the keeper, Oswald Partridge. He has promised to give my grandfather, Jacob Armitage, two dogs."

"Armitage?" said the gentleman. He looked at a paper in front of him. "Yes, I see he lives in the forest. Why has he not come to see me?"

"Why should he come to see you, sir?" asked Edward.

"Because I have been sent here to see what is happening in this part of the country. The King no longer rules it. All who work or live in the forest have been told to come here. I shall decide whether they may remain, or whether they must leave the forest."

"My grandfather has heard nothing of this, sir," replied Edward. "The King made him a keeper, but for two or three years he has received nothing from him. He has lived in his own house, which his father left him when he died."

"If he has received nothing, how does he live?" asked the man.

"He has some land, which gives us food; we have a horse and cart, and some cows."

"I know something about Jacob Armitage," said the man. "I know whose servant he has been. Now answer this question. You have come for two dogs. Do you need them to help you to work in the garden, or to feed the cows?"

"No, sir," replied Edward, "we need them to help us to find the deer."

"So you kill deer in the forest, do you? That is breaking the law."

"My grandfather has not killed a deer for three months," replied Edward. "He has been ill in bed. If he killed deer before then, and broke the law, he can be tried by an officer of King Charles, and by no one else."

"Your grandfather served under Colonel Beverley. I can see that he has taught you also to be a friend of the King."

"Sir," said Edward, "Colonel Beverley was very kind to my grandfather and to his father before him. They served him and honoured him. They did their duty to their master and to the King. I am ready to do my duty to the King, too."

"Colonel Beverley was a brave man. I honoured him," replied the gentleman. "But I serve the present government. I cannot let people remain in the forest if they are our enemies."

"Jacob Armitage owns his house and land," replied Edward. "You cannot take it from him. He can no longer follow the deer, or serve under you, because he is too old. But I came here to get two dogs. I suppose now that my journey is useless."

"No, you may have the dogs. They were promised to you. But I must tell you that you will break the law if you use them in killing deer. But I have no more time to waste. If you go to the kitchen, you will find something to make you feel refreshed after your journey."

Edward felt angry at being sent to the kitchen like a servant. But he thanked the man, and smiled at the girl, who had been standing near the table during his talk with her father. "Well," he thought, "I came here for two little dogs, and found a Roundhead." He went along a passage to the kitchen. He found no one there. In the garden he saw the little girl. She said, "I am sorry that there was no one in the kitchen to receive you. But if you will come with me, I will serve you."

Edward followed her. He was soon sitting before some very good cold meat and bread, which the little girl placed on the table. He thanked her, and began to eat.

"Will you tell me your name, please?" asked Edward.

"I am Patience Heatherstone, sir," she replied. "But now I must leave you." She went out, and Edward continued his meal. "She's a nice little girl," he thought; "she called me Sir. I cannot, therefore, look like Jacob's grandson, so I must be careful." Just then Patience returned and said:

"Oswald Partridge is coming now."

"Thank you," he replied. "May I ask one question? Where is the King now?"

"I have heard that he is living at Hurst, in the Isle of Wight," she replied in a low voice. "But it would be useless to try to see him. It would only hurt both him and you, if you tried to do so." She then left the room.

Seven

FIRE!

Edward finished his meal, and went to the back of the house, where he met Oswald. He told him the reason for his visit. "I did not know that Jacob had a grandson," said Oswald.

"I have only lived with him for a year," announced Edward. "I lived in the great house at Arnwood before that."

"Then I suppose you are on the King's side," asked Oswald.

"I would die for him," replied Edward.

"And I would, also. But come away from the house. We will go to the dogs' houses, where no one will hear us."

They went a little distance away, and Edward told him all that had happened that morning.

"This new *Intendant*[1] has brought some new keepers into the forest," replied Oswald. "But I am to remain. It will be difficult for you now to get venison to sell. I can give you the names of a few people who will buy from you, if you are willing to meet the danger of killing the deer. I shall come to see you the day after to-morrow. Take these two dogs. You must go now."

Edward got on his horse, which was tied near the gate of the house. He rode away across the

[1] Intendant = The chief officer in a forest. It is a French word used in Canada; the English word is Superintendent.

forest, with the two dogs following him. He had much to think about. Jacob could no longer help him very much; it would be dangerous to get venison from the forest now that the new keepers had come. But Humphrey's work in the garden and the fields would give them plenty of food. "If anything happens to me," he thought, "he will still be able to take care of my sisters. The King's friends are over the sea. If I go and offer to help them, Humphrey can remain here until I come back."

Late in the evening he reached home. He found that Jacob had been very ill the whole of the day. He was now asleep, and Edward did not wake him. The next morning, he told the old man all that had happened at the Intendant's house.

"You were very brave to tell him that you were ready to serve the King," said Jacob. "You must be wise and careful. I have not much longer to live. When I die, it will be your duty to take care of your sisters. Trust Oswald Partridge; I know him well, and he will prove to be your friend. When he comes here to-morrow, tell him that I am dying. I want to speak to him."

When Oswald came early next morning, he was much surprised to find that Jacob had four grand-children. After breakfast, he went into the bed-room where the old man was lying. There Jacob told him his secret. The children were the sons and daughters of Colonel Beverley, who people sup-posed were burnt in the fire at Arnwood. Oswald was delighted that Jacob should trust him so much. He came into the sitting-room. Then he bowed to Edward and said "I did not know who you were, sir. I am very glad to know that you and your sisters and brother are alive and well."

"But, Oswald," replied Edward, "remember that you must still call us Armitage. We are supposed to be Jacob's grandchildren."

"I will not forget, sir. I am glad that I know your secret. I may be able to help you. And now, I have to find some venison for the Intendant. Come with me. We may find enough for both houses."

They set out. Before darkness came, they had followed and killed two fine deer. It was too late to take any of the venison to Jacob, so Edward helped to carry it to the Intendant's house. When they arrived, it was quite dark. Oswald asked Edward to spend the night there, and return home the following morning. Edward was glad, for he might easily lose the way at night, when the forest was very dark.

"Now, Jane," cried Oswald to the servant, "can you give us anything to eat? We are very hungry."

"You shall be served at once," replied Jane. "I have bread and meat ready."

"And you must find a bed for my young friend, too," continued Oswald.

"There are no beds in the house, but there is plenty of good soft *hay*[1] in the room over the building where the horses are," replied Jane. "You

[1] Hay = Dried grass, used as food for cattle and horses.

must climb the *ladder* against the wall, but you will find a good bed when you get to the top of it."

After they had eaten their meal, Oswald, who lived a short distance away, showed Edward the place where he was to sleep, and went home. Edward climbed the ladder to the room over the horses. It had no door. The wind was so cold that he could not sleep. Although Jane had said that there was plenty of hay, there was not enough to cover him. After a little time, he came down into the yard, in order to get a little warmer. He thought that if he remained where he was, he would freeze. In the bedroom above the kitchen he saw a light burning. At first he thought it was Jane, the servant, going to bed. Suddenly he heard a loud cry. He saw the whole room brightly lighted. A woman was trying to open the window. Then he knew that the room was on fire. At once he ran to the ladder by which he had just climbed down into the yard. He brought it, and placed it against the wall of the house. He climbed to the window.

With one blow he broke the glass, opened the window, and jumped into the room. The bed and the bedclothes had caught fire and were burning brightly; he could see no sign of the woman. Then his foot touched something on the floor. It was the body of the Intendant's little daughter. He lifted her in his arms. His hands and face were burnt but he was able to carry her down the ladder. He laid her on the floor of the building in which he had tried to sleep. Her clothes were still burning, but he put out the fire with his hands. Then he ran out and shouted "Fire! Fire!" until the people in the burning house and the neighbouring houses ran out to help. Mr. Heatherstone came out half dressed. He saw that Edward had again climbed the ladder to the window of his little girl's room. He cried out to him to save her. But Edward was busy pouring water from the buckets which the neighbours were passing up to him. The shouting was so loud, that he could not hear a word that the Intendant said. He thought, too, that the people must have found where Patience was lying.

The Intendant cried "My child! My daughter! —burnt—burnt to death!" But the only answer he received was a voice from the crowd. It cried: "There were four burnt at Arnwood!" The Intendant tried to climb the ladder. The men held him back, for he could give no help to Edward. Then, thinking that nothing could save his daughter, he was led away to a neighbouring house.

Edward, with many willing helpers, at last put out the fire. He saw that there was no more danger, and came down the ladder. He called Oswald to him.

"Oh, sir," cried Oswald. "This is fearful. She was such a sweet young lady!"

"She is safe and well," replied Edward. "I brought her down before I tried to put out the fire. See, there she is. Cover her with your coat, and carry her to your house."

Oswald lifted Patience in his arms. Her eyes were closed. They reached the house and laid her on Oswald's bed. Then she opened her eyes. She looked around and cried, "Where is my father? Bring him to me!"

Oswald went out, and soon came back with Mr. Heatherstone. The Intendant was filled with joy to find his daughter safe and well. Father and daughter were alone when they met. Edward had left the room in which Patience lay: he joined Oswald.

"My arms are badly burnt, Oswald," he said. "Have you anything to put on them?"

"I will bring some oil," replied Oswald. He went into the house. He soon came back with some cloth and oil. With these he covered Edward's arms, which were now very painful.

"Mr. Heatherstone will want to thank you for saving his daughter's life," said Oswald.

"Yes," replied Edward. "For that reason I must ride home as fast as I can. You must not let him know where I live. He will want to thank me by offering me some kindness. I will receive no kindness from a Roundhead. I have saved his daughter's life, as I would save the daughter of anyone, even my enemy, from such a fearful death. But I do not want his thanks. Good-bye, Oswald. Come and see me when you can."

Edward rode fast. He wanted to get home as soon as he could. When he was about a mile from the house, Humphrey met him. Edward told him the story of how he had saved Patience from the fire. Humphrey then said that Jacob was very near to death. He had been asking to see Edward as soon as he returned. They both hurried home to the old man. They found him very weak and ill.

Jacob called Edward alone into his room, and said:

"Edward, I have a few last words to say to you. I am dying. Soon I must leave you to take care of your sisters. You will find some money in the wooden box under my bed. Be careful; do not get into trouble with the Roundheads who now rule the forest. If you can, stay here. The farm and garden will give you all that you need. Now call the children. I must say good-bye to them."

Humphrey and his sisters came in and knelt at the side of the old man's bed. He blessed them and asked them to pray for him. When they rose from their knees, he was dead.

Eight

COLONEL BEVERLEY'S SWORD

Jacob had been in his grave nearly six weeks. Oswald Partridge again visited the children. He was very sad when Edward told him of the old man's death.

"May peace be with him," he said. "He was a

good man. Tell me, are your arms quite well again?"

"Nearly well," answered Edward. "But why have you been so long away from us?"

"They have killed the King."

"Have they dared to do it?" cried Edward.

"They have," answered Oswald. "I heard some time ago that he was in London, and that he was to be tried."

"Tried! How could they try the King?" cried Edward. "By the laws of our country a man can only be tried by those equal to him in honour. The King has no equals!"

"Yet his enemies have tried him, and killed him," replied Oswald. "Two days after I saw you, the Intendant hurried to London. He did all that he could to stop this fearful thing, but could not. When he left, he ordered me not to leave his daughter alone. I could not come to you as I had promised."

Edward asked Alice to give Oswald some dinner. Then he walked into the forest. He felt that he must be alone.

"They have killed my king," he said to himself. "There was not a blow struck to help him. Not an arm was raised to guard him. Is there no honour, no brave spirit left in England? Yet, if I cannot hope to fight for my king, I can still fight against those who have killed him." But Edward knew that at present he was powerless, and that anger was useless. He returned to the house.

"I have brought Edward Armitage to see you."

Oswald told him that the Intendant had come back from London. He wished to see Edward, and thank him for saving the life of his child.

"I will take his thanks from you, Oswald. I have no wish to see him," answered Edward.

"But the young lady also wishes to see you. She says she will never be happy until she sees and thanks you. She made me promise that I would get you to do as she wishes. Her father will go to London in a few days. You can ride to the house and see her while he is away."

"Well," replied Edward, "perhaps I will go some day. But there are more important things to think about now." He asked Oswald many questions about the prices of different articles which were needed in the house. Oswald at once offered to go into Lymington with him, and help him to buy everything that was necessary. The horse and cart were soon ready, and they set out. They went to a small inn in the town. Oswald was a friend of the owner, who was, indeed, the man who bought the venison from Jacob.

"I have brought Edward Armitage to see you," said Oswald. "The old man is dead. His grandson will bring you the forest meat."

"That is good," replied the innkeeper. "I have not had any for some time. I suppose you are not one of the new foresters?" he continued, turning to Edward.

"No," replied Edward; "I do not kill venison for Roundheads."

"Right, my boy. The Armitages were all good true men. They served their King and the Beverleys well; but there are no more Beverleys to serve now, and no King."

In a short time, they arranged with the inn-keeper to supply him with venison. It would now be dangerous to bring it to the town; so Edward would come to Lymington to give notice to the innkeeper. The innkeeper would send men at night into the forest to bring it back. Edward and Oswald then bought the things they needed. They went to the gun-maker's house to buy powder and lead. Edward saw a *sword* hanging on the wall. He thought that he had seen it before.

"Whose sword is that?" he said to the man who was measuring out the powder.

"A servant of Colonel Beverley brought it to me to be cleaned," said the gun-maker. "Before any-one came for it, the house was burnt, and the whole family was killed. It was one of Colonel Beverley's swords. There is E.B. marked upon it. There is no one to pay me for my work. I do not know whether I should sell it or not."

"Well," said Edward. "My grandfather served Colonel Beverley all his life. I should like to take care of the sword. If I pay you for your work, will you let me take it? If one of the Beverley family ever appears, I shall willingly give it to him."

The gun-maker thought that Edward's offer was

quite fair. He received the money, and gave him the sword. Edward could hardly hide his joy. He hurried into the street.

"Oswald," he cried. "I would not lose this sword for a thousand pounds."

When they had finished all their business in Lymington, they loaded the cart, and got ready to return. Edward went into the inn to ask the innkeeper how much venison he would need from time to time. Oswald was standing by the side of the cart, when a man came up and looked at the sword.

"Why, that was Colonel Beverley's sword. I took it to the gun-maker to be cleaned."

"Indeed!" replied Oswald, "and who are you?"

"I am Benjamin White," replied the man. "I served at Arnwood until it was burnt down. Now I am working at the 'Fish' inn. How did you get this sword?"

Oswald told him how the sword had been found by old Armitage's grandson. "I never knew he had one," replied Benjamin. "But tell him that I should be glad to see him some day."

"I will," said Oswald. "I shall see him to-morrow."

Benjamin returned to his work; Edward came out of the inn, and soon they were on their way home.

"You must be very careful," said Oswald. "Benjamin knows you. If he sees you in Lymington, your secret will become known."

Nine

AN UNPLEASANT MEETING

Next day Humphrey asked his brother, "When do you mean to visit the Intendant's house, Edward?"

"In a day or two," replied Edward. "At present, I do not feel very kind towards Roundheads, although the young lady whom I have promised to visit is very friendly and kind."

"But, Edward, why do you feel more unfriendly to them now than usual?"

"I cannot forget that they have killed the King. I have another reason, too. In Lymington I discovered my father's sword. I almost think it is sent by Heaven. I mean some day to use it. Our brave father fought with it bravely for his King, and I trust that I shall draw it with as great honour as he did. Come with me, and I shall show if to you."

They went together into the bedroom; Edward brought out the sword, which he had placed by his side on the bed.

"See, Humphrey, this was our father's sword; I trust that I may draw it to fight for the King, and against those who killed our father."

"I trust that you will, my dear brother. But tell me how you found it."

Edward then told the story of all that had happened the day before at Lymington, not forgetting how Benjamin had appeared, and how he had arranged to sell their venison.

A few days later Edward made up his mind to pay the promised visit to Patience Heatherstone. He took his gun, called his dog, which he had named Holdfast, said good-bye to his brother and sisters, and set out on his journey across the forest. He did not take the horse, because Humphrey needed it for his work. He walked quickly, followed by his dog. He felt happy in heart as the summer air blew on his face. Soon more serious thoughts came to his mind. For some time he had heard nothing of what was happening outside the forest, or of how the Roundheads were treating the new King, Charles the Second. Then he thought of his father's death, the burning of Arnwood, and the loss of his lands. Then in a day-dream he thought of the years to come. He saw the new King leading his army against his enemies; he saw himself at the head of a company of horsemen, fighting bravely. He had won back Arnwood, and was building the house again in all its beauty.

Suddenly his dream was broken by a cry from Holdfast. The dog ran forward to meet a stranger. He was a powerful-looking man, dressed as a forester. Edward thought he had never seen such a bad and ugly face.

"What are you doing here, young man?" said the forester. He walked up to Edward. He held his gun ready in his hand.

Edward quietly raised his own gun, which was loaded. He then replied, "I am walking across the forest, as you can see."

"Yes, I see you are walking, and walking with a dog and a gun. Now walk with me. Deer-stealers are no longer allowed in this forest."

"I am not a deer-stealer," answered Edward. "I shall certainly not go with you."

"My orders are to take all deer-stealers, and I am sure you are one. Come with me."

"I tell you again I am not a deer-stealer. I am crossing the forest to the Intendant's house; do nothing foolish. You may suffer for it."

The forester saw that Edward meant what he said. He dared not try to force him to do as he wished. He gave way, and said, "You tell me that you are going to the Intendant's house. That is where I should have taken you if I had made you a prisoner. So walk on in front of me."

"No," said Edward, "I am not so foolish as to walk in front of a man with a loaded gun. But if you will drop your gun, I will walk by your side."

"You may walk by my side," said the forester.

They walked side by side for some time in silence. Edward watched the man carefully, for he felt that he could not be trusted.

At last the forester said, "Who are you, and why are you visiting the Intendant?"

"If you had treated me fairly," replied Edward,

"that would be a fair question. As it is no business of yours, I shall leave you to find out."

By this time, the forester began to think that he had made a mistake, and that Edward was some important person, dressed as a forester. He said, "I have only been doing my duty. I hope that you will forgive me."

Edward made no reply. When they arrived at the Intendant's house, he said, "Will you come in with me, or will you go to Oswald Partridge? Tell him that you have met Edward Armitage in the forest, and that I should be glad to see him. You are one of his men, are you not?"

"Yes, I am," replied the forester. "I shall go and tell him that you have come."

Edward turned away, and went to the door of the house. It was opened by Patience herself. She cried "Oh! how glad I am to see you! Come in." Edward took off his hat and bowed; Patience led him into the room in which he had first met the Intendant.

"And now," said Patience, holding out her hand to Edward, "I must thank you for saving me from a fearful death. I have been very unhappy because I could not thank you before now. How can I show you how thankful I am?"

"You have shown it already, madam," replied Edward. "You have given me your hand as a friend, and allowed me to enter your house."

"He who has saved my life becomes to me like a brother, whether he is a king or a ———"

"Forester," said Edward.

"I do not believe that you are a forester. My father also thinks that you have not always been a poor forester. He wishes to offer you better work than this, but he does not know what kind of work you would like to do. He has great power, although he has quarrelled with the rulers of the country because of the killing of the King."

"I have heard how he tried to stop them, and I honour him greatly," replied Edward. "Your father is in London, I believe, so I will remain no longer." He rose to leave the house; but Patience made him stay to eat the meal that she had prepared for him. Besides, she had a woman's curiosity. She wished to know more about this young man who had saved her life. Little by little she drew from Edward the story of his life at Jacob's house with Humphrey and his sisters. He carefully hid from her every real fact of his life at Arnwood. He told her that he had been taught to read and write there, and that Colonel Beverley meant to make him a soldier when he was old enough.

"If Colonel Beverley had been alive," he said, "and if the King still needed his service, I have no doubt that I should be serving under him now. But I have answered so many of your questions; may I be allowed to ask about yourself in return?"

Edward soon discovered that Patience was an only child. Her dead mother was the daughter of a great lord who in happier days had been a friend of

the King. For this reason, said Patience, the Roundheads doubted whether her father's feelings were
completely on their side. Cromwell, their leader,
did not trust him. He had sent him to this distant
part of England.

It was near time for Edward to return home.
Before he went, Patience asked him when he would
come to see her father, and receive his thanks.

"I cannot say," replied Edward, "perhaps some
day I shall be caught stealing deer. Then I shall
appear before him as a prisoner; and he will
certainly see me!"

"If you do kill the deer, no one shall hurt you.
Good-bye, then; and once more I thank you."

She held out her hand again to Edward. This
time he raised it to his lips. Then with a low bow,
he left the house.

Ten

EDWARD IN DANGER

As soon as he left the Intendant's house,
Edward hurried to find Oswald, who was waiting
for him.

"That Roundhead forester whom you met was
sure that you were a deer-stealer," said Oswald.
"But I told him that I often took you out with me,
and that the Intendant knew you. You could kill

all the deer in the forest after what you did to save his daughter from the fire."

"Thank you, Oswald," replied Edward, "but I can take no favours from Roundheads. Let them catch me if they can! But who is this man?"

"His name is James Corbould; he served in the army against the King, but he has been sent away."

"I do not like his face," said Edward.

"No, he does not look like a man whom you can trust. But I know nothing about him; he has been here only a week."

Edward remained that night with Oswald. Early in the morning he set out to return home. He walked slowly through the forest; he looked around from time to time for signs of the deer. At last he came near a little lake, where a deer might perhaps be lying in the cool shade of the trees. He called Holdfast to him. Then he went carefully on hands and knees through the long grass. Soon he came to an open space by the side of the lake. There was no deer there; instead, he saw the forester, Corbould, lying asleep on the ground. His gun lay near him; Edward gently lifted it, opened it, and took out the gunpowder. He was certain that the man could not be trusted.

He walked slowly homewards. About six miles from the house, he stopped to drink at a small stream. Suddenly he heard a low sound from Holdfast. At once he thought that Corbould had followed him. He looked up. About twenty feet away he saw Corbould standing behind a tree. His gun was pointing straight at him. There was a slight sound, but no explosion followed, for there was no powder in the gun. Corbould came from behind the tree, and struck at Holdfast with the end of the gun.

Edward ran towards him. "Stop!" he cried. "You tried to kill me. Now you are trying to kill the dog."

"I was trying to kill the dog, not you. I shall kill him if I get a chance."

"That is a lie," replied Edward. "If I had not taken the powder out of your gun, I should be a dead man now." He raised his gun and pointed it at Corbould. "Go back to where you came from. If you don't, I'll shoot."

Corbould saw that Edward meant what he said; he walked away until he thought himself to be out of danger from Edward's gun. Then he turned, and shouted "I'll kill you before many days are past." Edward remained until Corbould was out of sight. He then continued his journey homewards. From time to time he looked back to see if Corbould was following him. At last, just as it was getting dark, he saw a man running from tree to tree behind him. "Oh, you are there," thought Edward. "Well, I know the forest, and he doesn't. I will lead him round and round till he is tired of following me." He looked round. He saw that he was about half a mile from the place where a great hole had been dug many years ago by people in the forest. From this hole they had taken stones to build their houses.

It was now nearly dark; there was only the light of the stars. Edward walked on until he came to the open space round the hole. He looked round, and saw Corbould about a hundred yards behind him. He held Holdfast by the mouth, so that the dog could make no sound. Then he went on until the hole was exactly between Corbould and himself. He then began to run: Corbould followed him till he arrived at the hole. In the darkness, he could not see it, and fell head first into it. Edward heard the sound of Corbould's gun, and a loud cry of pain. "Well," thought Edward, "he can lie there all night. It will teach him a lesson, I hope."

He reached home late that night and told Humphrey and the girls his story. "I think I shall let him lie there for a day or two," he said. "Then I shall send to Oswald to let him know where the fellow is."

"But you say that you heard the sound of his gun," said Humphrey. "Perhaps he is wounded. He may die if he is left there."

"The best plan," said Edward, "would be for you to see Oswald to-morrow. Tell him what has happened, and show him where Corbould is lying."

Humphrey set out very early. Oswald was very angry when he heard Humphrey's story. He, too, thought that if the forester were left for a day or two, it would teach him a lesson. But at last he did as Humphrey wished. In the afternoon, he went with Humphrey and two other foresters to the hole. There they found Corbould in great pain. "Are you hurt?" cried Oswald.

"Yes, badly," replied Corbould. "I have shot myself in the leg. I have lost a great deal of blood."

It was difficult to lift the wounded man out from the hole. At last they did so, and laid him on the ground. Oswald and Humphrey returned to Jacob's house to bring a cart, to take Corbould to his house. As soon as they arrived, Edward met them.

"I shall tell the Intendant the whole story," said Oswald. "I have no doubt that he will send him away from the forest."

"No," replied Edward. "Let him tell his own story. He may be more dangerous if he is sent away. If he remains as a forester, we shall be able to watch him."

After a good meal, Oswald and Humphrey returned to the hole with the horse and cart. Very carefully the wounded man was placed in the cart; it went slowly through the narrow forest-paths. Every time the wheels went over a stone or into a small hole, Corbould gave a loud cry of pain. At last they reached Corbould's house, laid him on the bed, and sent for a doctor.

Humphrey said good-bye to Oswald, and drove back through the forest.

Eleven

DEATH IN THE FOREST

In the years that had passed since the Beverley children had come to live with old Jacob, we have followed the story of Edward. But many things had happened during this time to the other children, too. Humphrey had grown, like Edward, almost into a man. Since the death of Jacob, he had taken such care of the land around the house that it gave them nearly all the food that they needed. The money which Jacob had left to them had bought two cows which gave them plenty of milk. Edith and Alice had learnt to cook, to wash clothes, to keep the house clean. They did all the work needed by the little family. The garden was full of flowers in summer, and of fruit in autumn. Humphrey, with the help of Edward, had cut down the trees on a piece of land near the house. In this open space they had made a corn-field. From the branches of the trees they had made a fence for the field. Indeed, the place had become a fine little farm. Humphrey was proud of his work. He made up his mind that a farmer's life was the finest in the world. Alice and Edith, too, had almost forgotten their days in the great house at Arnwood. They enjoyed their work in the house and garden. They were busy all day, and just as happy as they were busy. But Edward was different. He was restless. He wanted to be a soldier, fighting for his king, and he felt that he was wasting his time as a forester. But the days passed, and no chance came for him to find the life which he most desired.

Some time after Edward's escape from being killed by Corbould, he went to visit Oswald. He wanted to find out what had happened to the man, so that he might guard against any danger to his life. Oswald told him that the Intendant had heard Corbould's story, but did not believe it. He thought that the forester had indeed tried to take Edward's life, but had not yet decided what to do with the man.

"I am sure that the Intendant does not believe you are Jacob's grandson," continued Oswald. "He means to visit you. And Patience knows that you have two sisters; she wishes to come with her father and see them."

"I cannot stop them coming, I suppose," replied Edward.

"No," said Oswald. "The Intendant has the right to visit every house in the forest. But I shall give you notice just before they come. Your sisters should be working in the house, and you and your brother in the field, on the day of their visit."

"All right," answered Edward. "Have you heard what is happening in London?"

"Three great lords have been tried and put to death for helping the King. Mr. Heatherstone went to London to try and stop the Roundheads killing them, but he could do nothing. King Charles the Second has been asked by the people of Scotland to come and rule them. He is now in France."

Edward was silent. The sad end of three good friends of the King brought his father's death back to his mind. Then the thought that the King might cross the sea to Scotland made him happier.

"Well," he said, "if the King does come, there will be plenty of work for a soldier to do. I shall join his army as soon as he lands."

As he went slowly homeward, Edward's mind was full of plans and hopes. That night he dreamt of life as a soldier. He fought battles at the head of a company of horsemen; he was saving the lives of Patience and her father from lawless soldiers. Next day he woke with such thoughts still passing through his mind. He took out his father's sword. He cleaned it until it shone like silver. Humphrey set out for Lymington to sell some eggs for Edith; Edward, his mind full of thoughts of war and a soldier's life, wandered into the forest, gun in hand, to find some venison.

He walked on, in a day-dream. At last he found himself in a part of the forest quite unknown to him. He had walked so far that it was already getting dark. He knew that he had lost his way.

"The best thing I can do," he said to himself, "is to walk in a straight line; I must then get out of the forest at last, even if I walk across it. That will be better than going backwards and forwards, or round and round. The stars will come out; then the North Star will guide me."

Suddenly, between the trees, he saw a light. He went forward quietly, and hid behind a large tree. About thirty yards away two men were kneeling on the ground by the side of a lamp which they had just lighted. Edward knew that the forest was the home of wandering thieves; some of them were old soldiers. After the war they had left the army and had no work to do. One of the men covered the lamp with his hat, so that no light could show.

Edward went closer; he heard one man say: "Are you sure that he has money?"

"Quite sure," the other man answered. "I looked through the window and saw him paying for the things that the boy had brought from Lymington. He took some pieces of gold from a bag."

"Well, we will first go to the front door, and say we are travellers who have lost our way. If they do not let us come in, you must continue talking. I shall go to the back of the house, and see whether the door or the window is open. Shall we start, Ben?"

"Yes," replied Ben. "A bag of gold is worth fighting for, Bill."

The two men rose up; Edward followed them. He was quite sure that they were thieves. He kept them in sight along the narrow forest-path; the wind was blowing, so that they could not hear the sound of his footsteps. At last they stopped. Edward saw that each man had a *pistol* in his hand, which he was loading. They went on again, until they came to an open space between the trees.

In the middle stood a small house. Everything was quiet. There was no moon, and the house was in darkness. Edward stood where he could see both the back and the front of the house. He could hear the man called Bill at the front door. He was asking to be allowed to enter. But the door remained closed, and a light shone under it. Then Bill began to beat on the door, and shout, as if he would force the people to open it. Edward knew, however, that he only meant to draw their attention from the back door, where Ben was trying to enter. Edward came nearer. He saw that Ben had opened the back window, and was standing by it with his pistol in his hand.

Suddenly there was a cry, "They are getting in behind." The man near Edward put his arm through the window and fired inside. Edward at once fired at the man. He fell. Edward loaded his gun again, and heard the front door being broken open. There was the sound of a shot, then all was silent. Edward ran round the house to the front door, where he found Bill lying. He entered, and saw another body on the floor. In its hand was held a pistol. A young boy was weeping over the body. "Don't be afraid; I am a friend," he said to the boy. He then took a lamp which stood on a table near him. He placed it on the floor in order to see whether the person was seriously wounded.

"Bring me some water, quickly," he cried.

The boy ran to bring the water. Edward found that the pistol-ball had struck the man in the neck.

Ben was standing by the window with a pistol in his hand

Blood was pouring from his mouth, and Edward could see that nothing could save the man's life. The dying man could not speak. He slightly raised his head, as if to look for the boy, who was now coming back with the water. When the boy again knelt by his side, the man pointed to him, and then looked at Edward. At once Edward knew what he wanted to say; he was asking him to take care of the boy. "I understand you," said Edward, "you want me to take care of your boy when you are gone? I promise that I will do so."

The man bowed his head, and a look of joy came into his face. He took the boy's hand, placed it in Edward's, and fell back, dead.

Twelve

A NEW FRIEND

In silence, Edward stood looking at the dead man, and the boy kneeling at his side. "What can I do?" he thought. "I must first find out whether these two thieves are dead or not." He took the lamp and went to the front door, where the body of Bill lay. He was quite dead, for a pistol-ball had passed through his head. He went to the back door, and heard a low voice saying, "Bill! Water! I'm dying!"

Edward put some water to the man's lips. He

drank deeply, and then said, thinking that Edward was Bill, "Tree—struck storm—mile north—dig—money—yours. Water!" He tried to drink again. As he did so, he fell back with a low cry.

Edward saw that he was dead. He went back into the house and shut the door. He lifted up the boy, who seemed hardly to know what had happened. Edward laid him gently on the bed in the next room. Then he looked carefully at the dead man. He was dressed simply, but his clothes were good. His hands were white, his beard carefully cut. He did not seem to be a workman, or farmer, or forester. "Ah!" thought Edward, "the family of Beverley are not the only people hiding from their enemies in the forest!" He then took the lamp and went to see the boy. He found him in a deep sleep. "Poor boy!" he said. "He has forgotten his sadness for a time. What a beautiful boy! I wonder who he is!"

Edward too was tired. Soon he had fallen asleep in a chair. When he woke, the sun had risen. He quietly opened the door, looked at the bodies of the two dead thieves; then he went outside. The night had been so dark that he had seen little of the space in which the house stood. All around was thick forest, which made the house a fine hiding-place. He wondered how he could find his way homewards. Then suddenly he heard the sound of a dog, and Holdfast sprang towards him. Behind him came Humphrey.

"Oh, Edward, how glad I am to find you. When

you did not come back last night, we thought you had fallen into some danger, and might be dead."

"But how did you find me?" asked Edward.

"I showed your old coat to Holdfast, and gave it to him to smell. I led him along until he found your foot-marks; then I followed him until at last he brought me to you."

"How far are we from home?" asked Edward.

"About eight miles, I think," said Humphrey.

Edward then told him in a few words what had happened, and led him into the house. The sight of the dead bodies surprised Humphrey. Soon the two brothers decided that Humphrey should return to Alice and Edith, and tell them that Edward was safe. He should then drive to the Intendant, tell him the whole story, and come back with the horse and cart. Humphrey set out on his journey, while Edward went to wake the boy, who was still lying on the bed.

"Come, you must get up now," he said. The boy sat up on the bed. For a little time he hardly seemed to know where he was. Then suddenly he remembered the fearful happenings of the night, and wept.

"I have lost my father," he cried, "he was the only friend that I had in the world. What will become of me?"

"I promised your father, before he died, that I would take care of you," said Edward. "You shall live with me and my brother and sisters, and you shall have all that we have. I have sent for a cart to take you to our home. Tell me, how long have you lived here?"

"More than a year," the boy answered.

"Whose house is this?" continued Edward.

"My father bought it when he came. He had escaped from prison. The Roundheads wanted to put him to death."

"Now listen to me," said Edward. "The Roundheads will steal everything if they find out that your father was a friend of the King. But we will load the cart with all things that we can move. Then we can take them to my house and hide them. The Roundheads will never know. You shall come with me this evening."

"You are very kind," replied the boy; "I will do all that you wish; but I feel very weak and ill."

After breakfast, the boy felt stronger. They began to gather together all the things to put into the cart. On the floor of the bedroom there was a heavy iron box, with a key, and several other cases. In the sitting-room were silver cups and dishes, pistols, two guns and a sword, with powder and balls. When Humphrey arrived with the cart, they filled it completely, and drove away. It was hard work to force the heavily loaded cart through the thick forest round the house. At last, however, they came to a good road. In less than two hours they were in sight of the house. Alice and Edith ran out to meet them. They were filled with joy to find Edward safe and well.

"I have brought you a play-fellow," he said. "Be kind to him, for he is very sad."

"We will make him as happy as we can," replied Alice. She took him into the house. Edward and Humphrey unloaded the cart, and carried everything inside. A few minutes later, Alice came running to Edward and cried:

"Edward, it's a girl!"

"A girl!" said Edward. "But why does she wear boy's clothes?"

"It was her father's wish. He dared not go into Lymington himself. He used to send her to buy things. He thought it would be safer if she was dressed like a boy. She says that she will tell me her whole story to-night."

Soon they were sitting at the table to eat their evening meal. When they had finished, Edward said with a smile, "I find that I have another sister instead of another brother. Now, will you tell me your name?"

"Yes; Clara is my name," replied the girl.

When they said their prayers that night, little Clara knelt and wept at their side. Alice and Edith tried to make her forget her loss. But their kind words and loving care only seemed to make her feel more and more sad; when they put her to bed, she cried until sleep came.

THE INTENDANT'S VISIT

The following morning, Edward and Humphrey went back to the dead man's house in the forest. They took the cart with them, in order to bring away the things that could not be put into it the day before. They were busy at this work, when Edward saw the Intendant, with Oswald and several other men, riding towards the house. Edward went up to him. He looked thoughtful and serious. He did not say a word about the danger from which Edward had saved his daughter. This surprised Edward, because Mr. Heatherstone and he had not met since the night of the fire. But Edward hid his surprise, and brought the Intendant and his *clerk* in silence into the house. He showed him the bodies of the two dead thieves and of Clara's father. The Intendant asked many questions, which Edward answered. His replies were written down by the clerk. When the Intendant understood all that had happened, he asked:

"Did you take away any papers?"

"I do not know," replied Edward. "The boxes that I took away were all closed, and I did not open them. I could not leave the boy here. Other thieves might have come."

"You should have taken nothing away," replied the Intendant. "The dead man is a well-known *Royalist*.[1] He broke out of prison a few days before

[1] Royalist = A man who fights for a king, or helps him in any way.

he was to be put to death. People supposed that he had escaped across the seas. His papers may tell us where other Royalists are hiding."

"Yes, and they may give you a chance to put to death some more brave friends of the King!" said Edward.

"Silence, young man! I will not allow you to speak such words against the men who now rule this country. I could send you to prison for using them."

"King Charles is my king," replied Edward. "My duty is to serve him, and not the men who put his father to death."

The Intendant took no notice of these words. He spoke to his clerk for a few minutes. Edward took this chance to leave the room. He called Humphrey aside. "When no one is looking," he said, "hurry home. Here are the keys. Look for all the papers you can find. Dig a hole in the garden and put the papers and the iron box into it."

Humphrey turned away. Edward went again into the house, and found the Intendant alone. He stood in silence before him, until Mr. Heatherstone spoke.

"Edward Armitage," he said, "I am sure that you have been used to a very different life from this. You are brave. You have saved my daughter's life, and for this I can never thank you enough. For your own good, I want to tell you that you are in danger. You must not speak such words as you have used against the Government. The forest is full of secret watchers. Even I have to be careful. It is well known that you are a Royalist. For this reason, I must appear to be unkind to you when other people are present. But my real feelings for you are the feelings of a father whose only child you have saved."

"Sir," replied Edward, "I thank you for telling me of this danger, and for your feelings towards me."

"I know I can trust you," said the Intendant. "This dead man, Captain Ratcliff, was my earliest and dearest friend. I knew his hiding-place. I tried to guard him, although he was a Royalist. I joined the people's party against the King only because he tried to destroy their freedom. But I have seen Cromwell, the new ruler of England, become as unjust as the King whom they killed. I have tried to hold them back; for this reason they no longer trust me."

"You may indeed trust me not to say a word," replied Edward.

"And now, one more question," said the Intendant. "You have surprised me by saying that you found a boy here. Captain Ratcliff had no son, but a daughter."

"I made a mistake, sir," replied Edward. "I did not discover that she was a girl until I took her home. I did not think that it was necessary to tell you, when your clerk was in the room."

"I am right, then," said the Intendant. "I will take her to my house and treat her as a daughter. Now remember, I must appear unkind and unpleasant to you when other people are present. But I know that you understand my real feelings towards you."

"I do, sir," replied Edward. Then they went out to join the other men of the party. Soon they were on their way to Edward's home. When they arrived, Humphrey met Edward, and told him in a low voice that everything was safely hidden. The Intendant and his clerk entered the house, and found Alice and Edith. They were at first rather afraid of so many strangers near the house.

"These are my sisters, sir," said Edward. "Where is Clara, Alice?"

"She was afraid, and went to her bedroom," replied Alice.

"You must not be afraid of me," said Mr. Heatherstone, looking curiously at the two girls. "I am only doing my duty. You have nothing to fear. Now, Edward Armitage, bring the boxes which you took from the dead man's house."

The boxes were brought and opened. The Intendant carefully looked into each box. Of course he found no papers. "I must send two of my people to help the clerk to look into the other rooms," he said. While they were doing so he asked that Clara might be brought to him. She came at once, for Alice had told her that there was no cause for fear.

"I was your father's dearest friend, Clara. You were not old enough to remember me, but you have often sat on my knee when you were a little child.

Will you come with me? I have a little girl three or four years older than you. She will love you dearly."

"May I come and see Alice and Edith sometimes? They have been very kind to me, and they call me sister," said Clara, with tears in her eyes. She was no longer afraid, for the Intendant had spoken kindly.

"Yes, you shall. My little girl will bring you here sometimes. I will not take you away now; you shall stay here for a few days. I will send Oswald Partridge to tell you when we shall come for you. And now, good-bye to you all."

The Intendant joined his people outside. As he was getting on his horse, he said angrily to Edward, "Take care! I shall watch you closely, for I doubt whether you can be trusted." He then rode quickly away.

"Why did he speak so angrily?" asked Humphrey.

"He doesn't want other people to know that he means to be kind to me," answered Edward.

The brothers had a long talk that night. Edward told Humphrey all that had happened during the day. When Humphrey knew that the Intendant really had friendly feelings towards Edward, he said:

"Perhaps he will help you to leave this place. I can take care of everything here, but you are wasted in the forest. You will serve the King better by going out into the world than by staying here and taking his venison."

"You are right," replied Edward with a smile. "I don't help him much by killing his deer. If the Intendant offers me work which I can do with honour, I shall take it. In that way, I may do something to help the King when he returns."

The next day, they dug up the iron box and a case in which Humphrey had hidden some of the dead man's papers. In the great box were bags of gold and jewels, worth many hundreds of pounds. They made up their minds to keep these for Clara, and give them to her when she grew up. The papers they meant to give to the Intendant, whom Edward felt he could now trust.

Fourteen

A PLEASANT PARTY

Three days later, Oswald Partridge appeared. The Intendant had sent him to say that he was coming with Patience the following day to take little Clara away.

"He is very pleased with you," he said to Edward. "He thinks that you are wasting your time as a forester. You should be doing work more fitted to your powers. He asked me many questions about you and your brother and sisters. I am sure that he thinks you are not the grandchildren of old Jacob."

"You must keep our secret, Oswald," replied Edward. "I like the Intendant more than I did, but I can trust no one."

"I shall never say a word, sir," replied Oswald.

Mr. Heatherstone and Patience came the following day. Edward helped the girl to get down from her horse. As she reached the ground, she held out her hand to him. Edward was surprised at this sign of good feeling towards a common forester, and he bowed.

"I wish to ask a favour," she said in a low voice. "If my father offers to help you in any way, please do what he asks. And now, let me see your sisters. My father has told me how nice they are." Edward took her into the house and left her with the three girls. He was very glad to see them become friends at once. Outside, he met Mr. Heatherstone. He arranged to take Clara away with him, together with all that she needed. He also took the papers which Edward had decided to give him. Humphrey went to load the cart.

"And now, Edward Armitage," said the Intendant, when they were alone, "I want to show my thanks for the service you have done to me. You were born for better things than to be a deer-stealer in this forest. I need a *secretary*. I know you will not serve the present rulers of the country. For this reason, I offer you work in my own house. I can pay you well. You will be near your family. You will be able to help them. I know that I can trust you, and I will send you from time to time on important business to my friends. You will then see the world and know what is happening. Think over the matter for a few days before you decide." Edward bowed; the Intendant went into the house.

Edward helped Humphrey to load the cart. They then went into the house, where they found a very pleasant party. Patience and the other three girls were laughing and talking happily together; to Edward's great surprise, the Intendant also seemed as happy as they. Alice and Edith had placed milk, cold meat, bread, cakes and fruit upon the table.

"I think your sisters are wonderful cooks," said the Intendant. "I have never tasted such good food. Your farm seems to give you everything you need!"

"Ah, but this is an unusual occasion," replied Edward. "Edith and Alice prepared for it. We do not have such food every day."

"No, I suppose not," replied Mr. Heatherstone, with a funny smile; "but if I opened the kitchen door, I might find something that you dare not show to the great Intendant of the New Forest."

"No, sir," replied Humphrey with a laugh. "For once you have made a mistake. Alice can cook venison as well as any cook in England, but to-day there is none in the house."

"Well, I must believe you," said the Intendant. "We have a long journey before us, and Clara is not used to riding."

They went out of the house, and after saying good-bye, the little party got ready to start. Just before they left, Patience bowed down from the horse and said to Edward in a low voice: "I hope you will do as my father wishes."

"I shall think about it," replied Edward. "I shall speak to Humphrey first. Then I shall decide."

"Very well," said Patience. "I am sure your brother thinks as I do, therefore I can hope." She then joined her father and rode away.

That evening, Humphrey and Edward talked a long time about the Intendant's offer. At first Edward thought that to sit at a table all day reading and writing would be very unpleasant.

"But did he not say that you would be sent on important business with his friends?" said Humphrey. "You will see the world. You will prepare yourself to become master of Arnwood when the time comes. Then you can make a fitting home for our sisters. Besides, you will be near Patience Heatherstone, who is a very sweet girl."

Before he slept that night, Edward thought long and seriously about the Intendant's offer. Humphrey's words stayed in his mind, and at last he decided that he would become Mr. Heatherstone's secretary. As he fell asleep he wondered how much the hope of seeing Patience every day had caused him to take what her father offered.

Fifteen

THE INTENDANT HAS A NEW SECRETARY

A week later, Oswald Partridge appeared at the door. He had been sent to bring Edward's answer to the Intendant's offer. He was glad to hear that Edward had decided to come as secretary.

"I am sure that Mr. Heatherstone will make your work pleasant," he said. "He really wishes to help you."

"Yes," replied Edward, "I shall be able to know what is happening in the country. Then I can prepare myself to join the King's army when he crosses the sea. Please tell the Intendant that I will come to-morrow to start my new work."

Oswald rode back. Edward gathered together the few things that he needed, ready to start early the next day. Humphrey was very pleased to hear that Edward had decided to join the Intendant, but Alice and Edith wept when the time came for him to leave them. The following day he rode across the forest. The Intendant received him with pleasure, and very soon they had arranged that Edward should begin his work. First, however, he had to get clothes more fit for his new work. His forester's dress would look strange at a secretary's table. He went therefore to Lymington, and bought some plain, grey clothes, and one of the tall hats which Roundheads used to wear. Humphrey, who had gone with him, smiled to see his brother in his grey coat and strange hat. "You are a real Roundhead," he said, "but you can hardly work for a Roundhead if you wear the bright colours and the feathered hat of a Royalist!"

"No," replied Edward, laughing. "People must think that I am a Roundhead until the time comes when I can change my hat!"

On his return, Patience and Clara ran to meet him. They showed him a large, bright room in which he was to live.

"I hope you will like your room," said Patience.

"Why, he never saw anything like it before," cried Clara.

"Yes, I did," replied Edward. "The rooms at Arnwood were much larger and finer." He turned and looked at Patience. She seemed to be trying to read his thoughts.

"Well," she said, "Arnwood was much finer, and your present house is much smaller. You have been used to larger rooms and smaller rooms, and I trust that you will be happy in this room."

"I should be hard to please," he replied, "if I could not be happy in a pleasant room like this. But although the rooms at Arnwood were finer, I did not say that they were ever mine."

Patience smiled and made no reply. They then left him to arrange the few things that he had brought with him. He looked around him, and thought how strange it was to find himself under the roof of a Roundhead. "And yet he knows my feelings, and I trust him," he thought. "Surely he cannot hope to win me over to his side? He has nothing to gain by doing so; I am a poor unknown

It was a very happy party that set out across the forest

forester. He remembers what I did to save his daughter; he is thankful, and shows his thanks in this way."

Perhaps, if Edward had asked himself the question, "Would I be so friendly with the Intendant if he had no daughter?" he would not have thought it so strange to find himself under a Roundhead's roof!

In a few days, Edward became quite used to life with Mr. Heatherstone and his daughter. In the morning he wrote a few letters for the Intendant; in the afternoon he could do as he pleased. He spent most of his time in the company of Patience and Clara. Once or twice Mr. Heatherstone asked whether he would like to go out with Oswald to kill a deer. He did so, and from the keeper he learnt that Corbould was well again, although he could not walk very well. The Intendant gave Edward a fine horse and he often rode with the two girls into the forest. Nearly a month passed very pleasantly, when Edward asked to be allowed to visit his family. Patience and Clara also asked to go. The Intendant gladly allowed them to ride with Edward. It was a very happy party that set out across the forest. Oswald had gone the day before to tell the girls that they were coming. When the party arrived, they found that Alice was cooking her best dinner, and that Humphrey was at home to receive them. Edith took Patience and Clara to see the garden and the farm, while Humphrey and Edward talked.

"You remember what I heard from the thief whom I shot," said Edward, "something about money that he had hidden?"

"Yes," replied Humphrey, "I remember now, but I had forgotten."

"Well, I have been thinking about it," said Edward. "The thief thought that I was his fellow-thief. He told me that the money was mine. But it was stolen, and I cannot take it. I think that everything which a wrong-doer leaves when he dies goes to the King. But I shall ask the Intendant about it."

"But, Edward," said Humphrey smiling, "what silly fellows we are! We don't know yet whether we shall find anything! But I shall look for the place, and see whether the thief spoke the truth."

"Do," replied Edward. "And now I am sure that dinner is ready. Let us go in."

They were very happy at dinner; and when the visitors set out to return home, Edith cried after them "Come again soon, Clara! Patience! you must come again soon!"

Sixteen

THIEVES IN THE FOREST

For some days Humphrey was very busy on the farm. He could do nothing about finding the thief's hidden money. At last, the chance came;

he remembered that the dying thief had spoken about a tree one mile to the north of Clara's house. He therefore set out towards the house with his horse and cart. He reached the trees which grew round the open space, tied the horse to a branch, and walked to the edge of the forest. He thought that it would be well to see whether everything had been left in order. The Intendant had given orders to his men to dig graves for the three bodies, to shut the doors and bring the keys to him.

As he drew near, he heard voices. He came closer, stepping very carefully. He hid behind a thick tree. The doors and windows of the house were open; outside the front door sat two men cleaning their guns. One of them was Corbould. The Intendant had sent him away when his wound had got better, and he was supposed to be in London. Three other men joined them. Humphrey stayed behind the tree for some time, but he was too far away to hear what they were saying.

"I am sure there is danger," thought Humphrey. "Corbould and the other men have no right to be living in that house. They must be some of the thieves that have been hiding in the forest."

He went quietly back to the cart, and drove it about a mile to the north. He looked carefully around until he saw a great leafless tree. "This must be the tree," he thought. "It looks as if it has been struck in a storm." Again he looked around near the foot of the tree. There was a little space where the grass was not so green as the rest.

He began to dig. After a few minutes' work, he struck something hard. He dug the earth away, and discovered the top of a wooden box. Soon he made a space all round it; he was able to lift the box out of the hole. He took it to the cart. As he was starting to drive away, he saw, at a distance of about two hundred yards, three men running towards him. They had guns in their hands. Humphrey called to the horse, and at once moved quickly away.

The men saw this, and shouted to him to stop. Humphrey replied by driving still faster. Then he heard the sound of a gun, and a ball came past his ear. Again and again the men fired, but by this time Humphrey was almost out of sight. "Well," thought Humphrey. "This is serious. These men are certainly thieves, and they will wonder what I have been digging up. I have no doubt that they know where I live. Corbould is sure to bring his band to the house and try to get the box. I must report this to the Intendant."

He drove as fast as the horse could go. He had left the girls at the house alone, in danger. The thieves had no horses. Humphrey hoped that he might see the Intendant and then reach home before the thieves could arrive. As he came near the Intendant's house, he saw Edward sitting in the garden. Hurriedly he told his story; Edward promised to get all the help he could.

"I don't think they will come before it is dark," said Edward. "I shall bring the men then, so that the thieves will not see us coming. We will catch them all, I hope. Guard the house well until we arrive."

Humphrey drove away. It was possible that the thieves might be daring enough to try and break into the house while it was still light; the girls were alone, and there was no time to waste. He drew near the house. Edith ran out to meet him, with a happy smile. He knew that the girls were still safe. Hurriedly he told Alice that they were in danger. The brave girl at once helped Humphrey to bar the doors and windows. Edith too helped them to pull the heavy chairs and tables from their places, and put them against the doors. Humphrey cut a few holes in the wood of the doors; Edith and Alice loaded the two guns which had been brought from Clara's house after her father's death.

There was no sign of the thieves, and it was now getting dark. They ate their evening meal in silence, listening for the smallest sound. Suddenly one of the dogs gave a low cry, and they heard a voice at the door. Was it a friend or an enemy?

"I have lost my way in the forest. May I stay here for the night?" said the voice. Humphrey knew that it could not be one of the Intendant's men. He shouted, "We never open the door at this hour of night. Go away." He took his gun in his hand.

There was silence. As Humphrey moved away from the door, a gun was fired into the key-hole.

But the strong bars held the door closed, although the gun had made a great hole in it. An arm appeared through the hole. The man tried to discover what was holding the door shut. At once Humphrey stepped forward and fired under the thief's arm. There was a loud cry, and the sound of a body falling outside.

"Here is another gun loaded," said Alice. She placed it in his hand, took away the one he had just fired, and loaded it again.

"Thank you, my dear," said Humphrey. "But go with Edith and sit near the fireplace; you will be safer there." The dogs continued to give low cries of anger. One of them was smelling under the back door. Humphrey went and fired through a hole which he had cut in the wood, but he could not hear whether he had hit anyone.

Suddenly a loud sound in Alice's bedroom told them that the thieves had broken the small window in that room. Humphrey had paid no attention to this window; he thought that it was too small for a man to pass through it. Humphrey called Hold-fast and Watchman, the two dogs, and sent them into the bedroom. Cries of anger and pain told him that they were struggling with the man who had entered. Both doors were now being beaten from outside by heavy pieces of wood. It seemed as if they would very soon give way. Humphrey fired again through each door. Suddenly other cries were heard outside; shots were fired and cries of anger arose.

"Those are the Intendant's men," cried Humphrey. "I am sure of it."

Then Humphrey heard Edward's voice calling his name. Soon they had pulled the tables and chairs away from the front door. They opened it.

"Are you all safe?" cried Edward. He stepped over the body of a man and came into the house.

"Yes, we are all safe," replied Humphrey. "Thanks to the help you have brought."

It was a joyful meeting of the brothers and sisters. Edward held the girls in his arms and kissed them. Oswald and some other foresters then came in, leading the prisoners whom they had caught. They went to Alice's bedroom and found a man half inside the window. He was held by the neck by the two dogs, and was quite dead.

"Corbould!" cried Oswald.

"Yes," replied Edward. "May heaven forgive him!"

They found that not one of the thieves had escaped. Corbould, and the man whom Humphrey had shot through the door, were dead. The prisoners were tied up and guarded. By this time the sun had risen. The Intendant's men ate the good breakfast that the girls prepared for them, and went off with their prisoners. Humphrey put the bodies of the two dead thieves into the cart and followed. He took with him the box which he had dug up from under the tree. When he arrived at the Intendant's house, he told the whole story to Mr. Heatherstone, and gave him the thief's box.

They opened it, and found forty pounds in gold, some silver and jewels.

"You have acted very fairly," said the Intendant. "I do not think we shall ever discover who owns these things. I shall keep them for you, and if the rightful owners do not appear, they will be yours."

Seventeen

EDWARD RIDES TO LONDON

A few weeks later, the Intendant called Edward into his room. "The King has landed in Scotland, and has gathered an army," he said quietly. "Sit down. We must talk a little on this subject."

Edward sat down. "At last," he thought, "my chance has come!"

"I suppose that now you wish to leave me, and join the King," said Mr. Heatherstone.

"I think that it is my duty, sir," answered Edward.

"Well, perhaps you will change your mind when you hear what I have to say. Your first duty is towards your family. Read these letters before you decide to leave them." He gave Edward three letters. They were written to the Intendant by friends of the King. Edward read them. He soon discovered that the King's English friends thought that the time had not yet come when they could do anything to help him. The army in Scotland was

really made up of the King's enemies. When they
had gained what they wanted, they would sell the
King to the Roundheads.

"I have shown how I trust you by showing you
these letters," said the Intendant. "There are
thousands of people who wish to see the King ruling
his country again. You know now that I am one of
them. But Cromwell is already marching northwards and he will cut this army to pieces. The
King's friends must wait."

"I thank you, sir," said Edward, "for trusting
me so completely. I shall always be guided by you.
I shall not leave you until you allow me to do so."

All happened as the Intendant had said. The
King's army in Scotland was beaten and destroyed.
The King hurried to a hiding-place in the moun-
tains. Edward felt that he had been wise to do as
the Intendant wished. He would never, he thought,
act against his wishes.

The days, weeks and months passed quickly and
quietly. Edward spent his time very pleasantly.
He went out with Oswald to shoot deer, and often
supplied venison to Humphrey and his sisters.
During the autumn, Patience and her father often
visited them; they sent them, too, presents of
flowers and books. Winter came. The snow was
so deep in the country roads that very few letters
came from London. One of them contained a
report that the King had escaped from Scotland,
and was gathering an army in Holland.

"I think, Edward," said the Intendant, "that

the time will soon come when we can help the King. When spring is here, I shall send you to London. There you will be able to judge what is happening; but you must be guided by me."

"I certainly will," replied Edward. "I want to strike at least one blow for the King."

A few weeks later, letters came reporting that the King was again in Scotland. He had been solemnly crowned, and large companies of his friends were joining him.

"This army is much stronger than the army that was beaten before," said the Intendant. "I shall now send you to London with letters to my friends. My servant Samson will go with you; you can send him back when you no longer need him. Lose no time. Cromwell is still in Scotland; I am sure that he is preparing for battle."

Edward had no time to say good-bye to his brother and sisters; but he sent Oswald to tell them that he was going to London. Clara and Patience promised to help him to prepare his clothes for the journey. He went up to his room. He took down his father's sword, which was hanging on the wall, and said aloud, "I hope that I shall use this with as much honour as my brave father!" He kissed it, laid it on the bed and turned round. To his surprise, Patience had come into the room unseen. He did not know that he had spoken aloud, and said:

"I did not hear you coming, Patience."

"Whose sword is that, Edward?" asked she.

"It is mine. I bought it in Lymington."

"But what makes you care for it so much? You kissed it before you laid it on the bed," she said. "You are a secretary, not a soldier. You should use a pen, not a sword."

"It was Colonel Beverley's sword; you know how kind he was to us," said Edward. "Remember I feel more fit for a soldier's life than for writing letters. If Colonel Beverley had lived, I should have followed him to the wars."

Patience made no answer. Clara joined them, and together the two girls gathered Edward's clothes and put them into the large bags ready for his horse. Edward went to see the Intendant. He received from him the letters which he was to carry to London, and also some money for his journey.

"If you leave London and join the King," he said, "it will be dangerous to write to me. Send Samson to me if you ride to Scotland; I shall then know that you have gone."

The following morning, before the sun rose, the sound of Samson's horse in the yard woke Edward. He was soon ready for the road. As he passed the sitting-room door, he saw a light in it. To his surprise, Patience came out of the room, and said:

"When I said good-bye last night, I forgot a little book which I meant to give you. Will you take it and read it? It is full of good thoughts, and it may help you sometimes."

"I will read it, and think of you," replied Edward.

"No, read it and think of what it contains," said Patience.

"Indeed, I will," replied Edward. "I shall not need a book to make me remember Patience Heatherstone."

He kissed her hand, and left the house. Soon he was riding a powerful black horse on his road to London. Samson followed close behind. On the evening of the second day, they drew near to the great city. Samson pointed out to Edward the different famous buildings that they passed. They reached a quiet inn, called "The Fox", where Mr. Heatherstone had told them to stay. Edward was tired with the long journey, and was soon in bed and asleep.

The following morning he looked at the letters which he had brought. One of them was for a certain Mr. Langton, at a house in Spring Gardens. Samson showed him the way. When they arrived, Edward was taken into a beautiful room filled with books. A tall thin man was sitting at a table. He was dressed in the dark clothes of a Roundhead. Edward gave him the letter. The man asked him to sit down while he read it.

"I am glad to see you, Edward Armitage," said Mr. Langton, after he had read the letter. "I find that Mr. Heatherstone trusts you completely. He says you may be going to the North of England, and that you will take any letters I may have to send. I will prepare them for you." He then asked many questions about his friend the Intendant, and his daughter, which Edward answered. He then went on, "Are you going to stay many days in London?"

"I shall be guided by you, sir," said Edward.

"Well, these are dangerous times. London is full of men whose work it is to watch all new-comers. You should leave London as soon as you can. To-morrow I will send you letters to some friends in the North. They will help you."

Edward rose to leave, and thanked Mr. Langton for his kindness. He then took the other letters to the people to whom Mr. Heatherstone had written them. The most important letter was to a mer-chant. This man arranged that Edward should be able to receive whatever money he needed from another merchant in York. The other letters were to friends of Mr. Heatherstone, who all received Edward with kindness, and promised to help him, if help was necessary. Edward then felt that there was no reason to remain any longer in London. He told Samson to return to the Intendant the following day. Then he prepared for his own journey, went to his room, and slept.

Early next afternoon the letters which Mr. Langton had promised were brought to him. As soon as he received them, he said "Good-bye" to Samson, and rode out of London on the Great North Road.

Eighteen

THE GREAT NORTH ROAD

An hour or two later, as the sun was setting, he arrived at Barnet, and decided to go no further. There was only one inn in the place. Here he stopped. He attended to his horse. He then went into the large room where travellers usually sat. He wore the dark clothes and tall hat which he wore when he was Mr. Heatherstone's secretary. When he entered the room he saw three men sitting by the fire. They looked at first like gentlemen, but their fine clothes were dirty and worn. They looked up as Edward brought his bags into the room. One of them said:

"That's a fine horse you were riding. Is he very fast?"

"He is," answered Edward. He turned away to speak to the innkeeper's wife. He gave her his bags to take care of. He did not like the look of the three men.

"Are you going north?" said another of the men.

"Not exactly," replied Edward. He walked across the room to the window. He wished to escape from any more talk with the men.

"This Roundhead is very proud," the third man said, in a loud voice.

"Yes," shouted another. "It is easy to see that he is not used to being spoken to by gentlemen; for twopence I would cut his ears off."

Edward took no notice, for he did not wish to quarrel with the men. The innkeeper came in. He ordered the three men to leave the inn. At first they would not go. Then the innkeeper said: "If you don't go at once, I'll send for someone who will throw you out!" They looked angrily at him, but went.

"I am sorry, young master, that these fellows were here. I did not know that my wife had let them come in. We know well who they are; but we can prove nothing against them. If you are going far, you should not travel alone."

"Thank you for telling me," said Edward. "I thought that they looked like *highwaymen*."

"You are right, sir," replied the innkeeper. "I only wish we could prove the fact. In these troubled times, we innkeepers have to take in all sorts of doubtful people. But you have a good sword there. Have you got any pistols?"

"I have," replied Edward, opening his coat and showing them.

"That's right. I hope that you may not have to use them," said the innkeeper.

As soon as he had eaten a late meal, Edward took his bags and went to his room; soon he was asleep.

Early next morning he went to see his horse being fed. The three men were standing near, but they said nothing to him. He returned to the inn, and called for breakfast. When he had finished, he took out his pistols, and loaded them with fresh powder. As he was doing so, he looked up. He saw one of the men with his face against the window, looking into the room. "Well," thought Edward, "now you see what you may expect if you try to cut my ears off!" When he had paid the inn-keeper, he rode away. Just after he left the town, the three highwaymen rode past him from behind.

He had ridden slowly for about fifteen miles, when he came to a wide treeless space. He rode on faster, and saw in front of him the three highway-men. They were riding down a hill which was between him and them. For a time he lost sight of them.

Edward stopped his horse to give him a little rest, then rode slowly up the next hill. He had nearly reached the top, when he heard the sound of a pistol, and a man came *galloping* towards him. He had a pistol in his hand, and his head was turned back. Behind him came the three highwaymen. One of them fired his pistol, but he missed the man in front. The man in front fired in return, and one of the highwaymen fell from his horse. All this happened so suddenly that Edward hardly had time to draw his own pistol. The man passed him, then the two highwaymen. Edward fired; the second thief dropped to the ground; the third man turned his horse and galloped across the fields. The horseman to whose help Edward had come stopped and rode up to him.

"Thank you for your help, sir," he said. "These three thieves were too many for me to deal with. I was riding north when they came up behind me. I looked round and saw at once that they meant to stop me. I turned my horse off the road towards some trees. One of them rode forward to stop me, and the others went to the further side of the trees to get behind me. When I saw that they had separated, I rode back again as fast as I could. At once they followed me. If you had not been here to help, I should now be a dead man."

"What shall we do with them?" asked Edward, pointing to the two bodies on the road.

"Leave them where they are," replied the stranger. "I have important business in the North, and I cannot waste time over two dead thieves."

Edward too wished too hurry onwards, and they made up their minds to travel together. The stranger seemed to be a well-mannered gentleman, and Edward soon began to like him. He was a strong, good-looking man of about twenty-three years of age. He was dressed richly, with the Royalist hat and feather. As they rode northwards, they talked of many things. Neither the stranger nor Edward said a word about the business which was taking them on their long journey. All they knew about each other was their names. They kept away from large towns; the stranger said that he did not wish to be watched, and Edward felt exactly as his new friend did. They stopped at night at small inns in villages by the roadside.

Thus they continued their journey for several days. At last the stranger said: "Master Armitage, we have travelled together for nearly a week. We know nothing of each other's plans. But if you can trust me, I feel that I can trust you. By your dress I suppose you to be a Roundhead; but your manners are those of a gentleman. I think a hat and feathers would be more fitting to your head than that ugly thing that you are wearing."

"Indeed, Mr. Chaloner," replied Edward, "you are right. If I could, I would willingly change my dress."

"I believe you," said Chaloner. "Is not your business the same as mine? I am riding to join the King. I believe you are really a Royalist. I can take you with me to some friends. They will let us stay with them safely. The chance will come to strike a blow for the King."

"Who are your friends?" asked Edward.

"Their name is Cunningham," replied Chaloner.

In silence Edward took from his coat the letter which Mr. Langton had given him. He gave it to Chaloner, who read "To Miss Cunningham, at Portlake, near Bolton."

Chaloner laughed aloud. "This is fine!" he cried. "Two people meet. They are going to the same place, on the same business; and for nearly a week they dare not trust each other."

"In these dangerous times, a man never knows whom he can trust," said Edward.

Chaloner then spoke about the struggle which

would soon begin between the King and Cromwell. He said that the Royalist army was gaining strength every day. It was well supplied with all that it needed. Thousands of men would join it when it marched southwards into England.

"My father was killed at Naseby," he went on. "All that he had was taken by the Roundheads. If I did not receive money from my good old aunts, I should have nothing."

"Your father fell at Naseby?" said Edward. "Were you there?"

"I was hardly more than a boy," replied Chaloner, "but I fought at my father's side."

"My father also fell at Naseby," said Edward.

"I do not remember the name—Armitage?— was he in command there?"

"Yes, he was," answered Edward.

Chaloner looked at him doubtfully. "There was no officer named Armitage at Naseby," he said.

"I have spoken the truth," replied Edward. "You have shown that you trust me. I will trust you. My name is not Armitage. It is Beverley. My father commanded a company of Prince Rupert's horsemen at Naseby."

Chaloner was greatly surprised. "Indeed, when I first saw you I thought that you looked like some-one whom I used to know. You are very like your father; he was a fine soldier, and I honoured him. We must be friends, Beverley."

"Indeed, we are," replied Edward. He then told Chaloner the story of his escape from Arnwood, and his life as a forester. When he ended, Chaloner said: "We heard of the fire; everyone believed that you had all been killed. But, if you had not met me, did you mean to join the army as Armitage or as Beverley?"

"I hardly knew what to do," answered Edward. "I wanted a friend to guide me."

"You have found a friend in me," said Chaloner. "When you meet the King, you must tell him your real name. Your father was the best soldier in King Charles's army. His son, our new king, will remember him well. We are near the end of our journey now, and my aunts will think themselves greatly honoured to have a Beverley in their house."

Late that night, they arrived at Portlake, a fine old house built among beautiful trees. In the hall two old ladies met them. They were delighted to see Chaloner, who was their sister's son. At first, they looked rather doubtfully at Edward in his Roundhead dress, even when he gave them the letter from Mr. Langton. Chaloner then told them that he was the son of Colonel Beverley, and told the story of the highwaymen. They then received him with the greatest pleasure.

After the evening meal, Chaloner asked whether any letters had come for him. One of the·ladies brought several letters. Chaloner read them, and gave them to Edward. They were from *General*[1] Middleton and other friends with the King's army. From them they learnt that the King's army had

[1] General = A very high officer in the army.

Late that night they arrived at Portlake

marched southward secretly. It was now between Cromwell and London. Hundreds of the King's English friends were joining it.

"Where is the army now?" asked Edward.

"They will be only a few miles away from us to-night, for they are marching fast. To-morrow we can join them."

Nineteen

THE KING'S GUARD AT WORCESTER

Before they left their beds the next morning, a letter arrived from General Middleton. Chaloner and Edward learnt that the army had rested during the night only six miles from Portlake. They dressed hurriedly. Then Chaloner said, "It will seem very strange if a Roundhead marches up to the King and says that he is Colonel Beverley's son!" In a few minutes, with the help of some of Chaloner's clothes, Edward was changed into a fine-looking Royalist soldier, complete with hat and feather. An hour's ride brought them to the General's tent. He received Chaloner as an old friend; when he heard that Edward was the son of Colonel Beverley, he said that King Charles would be happy to see him. The General took them to the King's tent. They waited outside for a few minutes. Then an officer came out. He said: "The King will see you now." They entered the tent.

"Sir, I have brought the sons of two of your bravest officers," said General Middleton to the King. "This is John Chaloner. His father was killed at Naseby."

"I have no doubt that the son is as brave as his father," replied the King. He held out his hand. Chaloner knelt on one knee and kissed it.

"And now, sir, I have a surprise for you," said the General to the King. "This gentleman is the son of Colonel Beverley, who also gave his life at Naseby."

"Indeed," replied the King. "I heard that all the family was killed at the burning of Arnwood. Young man, your father served my father well. How can I show my thanks to his son?"

"By allowing me to be near you when you are in danger, sir," said Edward.

"That is the answer that I expected from a Beverley," said King Charles.

Edward and Chaloner then left the tent. A few minutes later the General joined them. "The King has made you a captain," he said to Edward. "He has given orders that you should be always near him."

In a short time Edward was ready to join the company of King's Guards. The army marched quickly southward to Warrington, where they met a company of Cromwell's horsemen. The Round-heads were easily driven off the field. The King's army was filled with joy. They thought that they had beaten Lambert, one of Cromwell's best generals. But Middleton knew that this was only a small part of the Roundhead army. Cromwell himself was marching to the south with most of his soldiers. He meant to get between the King and London. In this way he would stop King Charles from joining his friends in the South of England.

Then reports began to come of serious losses in the North. Lord Derby and some other officers had been left behind to gather together companies of soldiers to join the King. They were marching southward a hundred miles behind the King's army. They were taken by surprise at Wigan. Many were killed or taken prisoners.

"This is a serious matter," said Chaloner. "We have lost our best officers. The generals are quarrelling among themselves about the chief command of the army. Middleton is the only general who is doing his duty well."

The King wished to march quickly to London. But the soldiers were tired with the long march. The weather was very hot, and they could go no further without resting. The leaders decided to march to Worcester, a town friendly to the King. Here they stayed for five weeks. The generals continued to quarrel. The soldiers were tired of doing nothing and began to leave the army. Reports came in that Cromwell's army was becoming stronger every day. It was marching to Worcester. Still no one tried to make any plan to meet the danger. At last a report came that Cromwell was only five miles away.

That night and the following morning, Edward rode with the King to see whether the army was ready for battle. They found most of the officers and men sad and hopeless, but willing to fight. At noon, the King returned to his house. Before an hour had passed, the battle began. The King rode to the chief gate of the city, with Edward and other officers of his guard. Before they could pass through the gateway they were driven back by a great crowd of Royalist soldiers. Nothing could stop them. The King called their officers by name. They paid no attention. Such fear spread through the crowd that in its desire to escape, the King and his guards were nearly thrown from their horses.

Cromwell had sent his horsemen across the river. The watchmen on the city-walls were so careless that they had not seen this movement. No one expected him on that side of the town. He easily drove back the Royalist horsemen; some of the officers fought bravely, but their men would not help them. Many were taken prisoners; others ran away.

The King rode back into the town. Chaloner had gathered a few horsemen, and was prepared to fight. "Follow me," said the King. "We must try to stop this foolish fear from spreading." He galloped away, followed by Edward and Chaloner and several men of his guard. But he soon found that the other soldiers were unwilling to help. He rode on. Chaloner at last knew that the King's life was in danger. The battle was lost. "Sir," he said, "you must escape. The army is no longer fit to fight, and the Roundheads are following us fast."

King Charles would allow no one to go with him. He did not wish to bring his friends into danger; that night he rode away alone.

The next morning that part of the King's army which had escaped from Worcester discovered that the King had left them. The soldiers then separated into small companies, and slowly returned to their homes in the North. Bands of Roundheads spread over the country to try to take them. They made many prisoners; many, however, escaped. Among them were Edward Beverley and John Chaloner.

Twenty

ONCE AGAIN IN THE FOREST

Two days later the two friends were riding slowly uphill along a narrow road. "Well," said Edward. "This is a fine end to my hopes of fighting for the King! I haven't struck a single blow for him yet!"

"That is true," answered Chaloner. "The only danger is to get back to our own homes. If you are going to the New Forest, may I go with you? Cromwell's army will be marching northwards to take the Royalists who escaped. They will go to

Portlake, I am sure. I dare not return there. It will be safer for me in the South."

"Yes, come with me," said Edward. "We can find a hiding-place in the forest. Then we can decide upon some plan. But listen! That was the sound of a gun." They rode on over the top of the hill. About half a mile away they saw a little company of Royalist horsemen fighting hard against a larger band of Roundheads.

"Come, John," cried Edward. "Let us strike at least one blow." They galloped up to the fight. The Roundheads, thinking that the two horsemen were leaders of a larger company, soon gave way and rode off the field. They left ten of their men dead or wounded on the ground.

"Thanks, Beverley! Thanks, Chaloner," cried a young man. It was Grenville, one of the King's Guard, whom they knew well. "These fellows of mine were just going to run away when you came up. I shall stay with them no longer; I shall join you if you will allow me." He told the men that it would be safer for them to go to their homes separately. They went away gladly.

"We must do what we can for these wounded men," said Edward. "Then we can take the clothes of the dead men and dress ourselves in them. We shall pass through the country safely, because people will think we are Roundheads."

Grenville and Chaloner thought that this was a very good plan. They tied their horses to a tree. They attended to the wounded men, dressed them-

selves in the clothes of three of the dead Roundheads, and rode away. When it was getting dark,
they came to a small inn.

"We must be very bad-mannered; then people
will think that we are Cromwell's soldiers," said
Grenville. They went into the inn. They soon
found that people were very much afraid of them.
Everyone thought that they were a band of Roundhead soldiers seeking for Royalists who had escaped
from Worcester. Edward ordered the best food to
be brought. They slept in the best room in the
inn, and rode away the following morning without
paying a penny. In this way, they continued
their journey to the New Forest. Wherever they
stopped, people had no doubt that they were men
of the Roundhead army. Thus they passed safely
through the country, although bands of soldiers
were busy seeking all the King's friends who had
escaped after the fight at Worcester.

Edward then planned to escape from England
with his new friends. He meant to take them to
Humphrey's house and hide them. Then he would
go to the Intendant, dressed as a Roundhead
soldier. People would therefore never think that
he had been with the King's army.

A week after the battle, they drew near the
forest. Edward guided the little party to the house.
It was nearly dark when they arrived. Humphrey
was in the yard when he heard the sound of the
horses' feet. At first he ran towards the house to
bar the doors, but the voice of Edward soon set

his mind at rest. He and the girls were filled with joy at his return; soon the three friends were seated at their evening meal. Edward arranged to visit the Intendant the following day; he meant to tell him the whole story of the last few weeks, and ask him what he should do.

The next morning, before Chaloner and Grenville were awake, Edward rode across the forest. At the gate of the Intendant's house he saw Oswald. For some time the keeper did not know him in the dress of a Roundhead soldier. Edward called to him, and at once Oswald knew the voice. Edward then told him how he had escaped by changing clothes with one of the enemy.

"I will take care that people will think that you have been fighting for Cromwell," said Oswald. "You should wear these clothes all the time."

Edward went into the house, and met the Intendant. Mr. Heatherstone was greatly surprised to see Edward in his strange dress. "My dear Edward," he said, "I am glad to see you in any dress. Sit down and tell me all." Edward soon told him what had happened, how he had escaped and why he was dressed as a Roundhead.

"It is dangerous to remain here," said the Intendant. "Very soon it will be known that you fought, not for Cromwell, but for the King. Your friends will be in danger too. Hide them for a few days. No one ever visits your place. But you must arrange to cross the sea as soon as you can. And now, you will find Patience and Clara waiting for you."

Edward left the room. The two girls received him with great pleasure. They knew nothing of what had happened to him in the past weeks. He told his story. Patience nearly wept when she heard of the dangers through which he had passed. But her tears soon changed to smiles; she was happy at his return, but sad when he told her that he must soon cross the seas.

Twenty-one

TWO SECRETS

The days passed. Edward learnt that the King was still free. All over the South of England, parties of Roundhead soldiers were seeking for him. Edward's two friends were still safe with Humphrey and his sisters. One day Chaloner said to him, "It is very sad that Alice and Edith should live here in the forest. They are beautiful girls. They should be in a king's court."

"Yes," replied Edward. "I cannot forget that they are Colonel Beverley's daughters. But what can I do? I am sure that Arnwood will be given to some Roundhead; I shall always be a poor man. They must remain here, and work like the daughters of a forester."

"I have a plan," said Chaloner. "My aunts at Portlake are rich. They are alone in the world. I am sure that they would be very happy to take care of your sisters. You saved my life; they would

love to do something in return. May I write to
ask them?"

"I thank you, John," answered Edward. "I
know that your aunts would take good care of
them. They will be safer at Portlake when I have
gone. Will you let me know what your aunts reply
to your letter?"

"I shall do so," said Chaloner.

Just then, a party of horsemen rode up to the
house. Humphrey was working on the farm;
Edward met them at the gate. The officer in
command asked him who he was.

"I am the secretary of the Intendant of the
forest, sir," answered Edward. "He sent me here
with two soldiers. They will stay in this house at
night. During the day they will ride through the
forest to look for any of the Royalists who have
escaped from Worcester. We have heard that some
of them are trying to cross the sea, and that they
are hiding in the forest. Do you wish to see the
two men, sir?"

"No, I cannot wait," said the officer. "Forward!
men," he continued. The soldiers rode quickly
away, and in a few minutes they were out of sight.

For two or three weeks the Roundhead soldiers
continued to ride through the forest. Several times
they visited the house. Each time Edward showed
them a letter which the Intendant had given him.
In this letter Mr. Heatherstone ordered him to be
on the watch to take the King or any Royalist who
might be hiding in the forest. The Roundhead

officers were quite satisfied with this letter. They
rode away believing that Edward and his friends
had been sent into the forest on the same business
as themselves. At last there was not a party left
in the forest. They had all gone to the sea-coast
to stop Royalists from escaping to France.

Edward thought that it was now time to arrange
his own escape. He knew that he would never be
safe in England. For a time he might hide in the
New Forest; but it was certain that the Roundheads would never rest until they had taken all the
Royalists who had been near the King at Worcester.
He therefore rode over to the Intendant's house to
ask him what he thought it best to do. He found
him sitting at a table reading a letter. In silence he
gave it to Edward, and smiled. Edward read it.
He learnt that the Government was very pleased
with the services of the Intendant in seeking for
Royalists who had fought at Worcester. In return
for these services, they granted him the lands of
Arnwood. Edward laid the letter on the table.
He could not speak. "This is the end of all my
hopes," he thought. "I shall never own my father's
lands." He looked at the Intendant's face. Mr.
Heatherstone was still smiling.

"Edward," he said. "Ever since I first saw you,
I doubted your story. I could see that you were
born a gentleman, and not a forester. Then I met
your sisters and brother; I could see that they
too were not foresters' children. One day I was
in Lymington. By chance I met a man named

Benjamin, who had been a servant at Arnwood. I asked him many questions. He believed that you were all burnt to death at Arnwood; but he gave me the names and ages of Colonel Beverley's children. He told me what they were like. I decided that there could not possibly be two families of the same age and the same names. Tell me, Edward, am I right? Are you not Edward Beverley?"

Edward saw that his secret was known. It would be useless to hide the fact any longer. "Sir," he replied, "I am Edward Beverley; but now I shall never be master of Arnwood."

Mr. Heatherstone laughed aloud. "Do you really think that I should take what rightly should be yours? I certainly planned to get Arnwood granted to me. But I did so in order that it should not fall into other people's hands. Some day, I hope that the King will return. You know that I am one of the persons who are working secretly to help him. If the King returns, it will be safe for all the world to know that you are Edward Beverley. Arnwood will be yours. If he never returns, I shall hold it for you, and send money to you across the seas. The Government will never know the trick which I have played upon them."

Edward stood silent. He did not know how to thank the Intendant. At last he spoke. "At first," he said, "I thought that you were unjust in taking Arnwood from the hands of people who have no right to possess it. But now I know that you really

are my friend. I thank you for your goodness to
me and to my sisters and brother. You have told
me your secret, and trusted me. You know one of
my secrets, but I wish to tell you another."

"Yes, Edward," said the Intendant, "but I
think I can guess it. Has it anything to do with
Patience?"

"Sir, I love your daughter," answered Edward.
"I have never dared to tell her. I could offer her
nothing but the life of a forester's wife. Even now,
I must leave England. If the King escapes, I must
wander with him in strange lands. I cannot ask
Patience, even if she loves me, to go with me to
such a life."

"I do not think you need doubt her love," said
Mr. Heatherstone. "A father knows a motherless
daughter's feelings. I know by a thousand little
signs that Patience loves you."

Edward was filled with joy. He had never
dreamt that he could ask Patience to be his wife.
The Intendant's words gave him new hope. "I
shall see her at once," he said. He went into the
garden. Patience was sitting there reading. She
looked up, and read his secret in his eyes. "You
are going across the seas," she said, "but you will
come back; and when you come back, you will
find me waiting for you, Edward Beverley."

Twenty-two

THE KING'S RETURN

A few days later, Chaloner received a reply from his aunts. They would gladly receive Alice and Edith in their home, and treat them as their daughters. Soon everything was arranged for their journey to the North of England. The girls were very sad. They were leaving their brothers, whom they loved dearly, to go to strangers. But Edward soon showed Alice that his plan was for their good. With Edith he had a more difficult task. She was leaving not only her brothers, but her cows, her horse and her hens; these animals were friends too.

Humphrey drove the girls into Lymington, where he bought a carriage to take them to London. There they arrived safely, and found Miss Cunningham's own carriage waiting for them. Humphrey gave his sisters into the care of two old servants; they started on the journey to Portlake with many tears. Humphrey returned to the New Forest.

The Roundhead soldiers had now ceased hoping to take any more Royalists on the South Coast. After saying good-bye to the Intendant and Patience, Edward, with his two friends, Chaloner and Grenville, set off to Southampton. There they received letters secretly from France saying that at last King Charles had escaped. He was in Paris, and many of his friends were joining him. They sailed in a small fishing-boat, and with a good wind, reached France safely.

Thus the Children of the New Forest were separated. Humphrey alone remained to work on the farm. His sisters and Edward were far away. Would they ever come together again? No one could say. In the North the girls lived quietly and grew into beautiful young ladies. No one but Chaloner's aunts knew their story. In France, Edward became a soldier, like many other friends of the King. At first he fought in the armies of France. Later, Cromwell's Government became friendly with the French, who made King Charles leave their country. Edward went with him to Spain and Holland; Chaloner, Grenville and Edward became known as the bravest of the little band of Englishmen who were ready to serve their King with their lives.

. . . . .

Cromwell died in 1658. For a short time his son Richard tried to rule. But England was tired of Roundheads and their rule; two years later a large band of gentlemen crossed to Holland and asked the King to return to England.

It was early summer. The sun shone down on great crowds that filled the London streets. The windows of the houses on both sides were filled with ladies. They waved their jewelled hands to the King as he rode past. At his side rode Edward, Chaloner and Grenville, who were his most favoured servants.

"Look, Edward," said Chaloner, "do you know those two beautiful girls sitting at that window?"

"Indeed I do not. Are they two of the court ladies who have come from France to attend on the Queen?"

"Why, you are a fine brother! They are your sisters," cried Chaloner with a laugh. "There are my two aunts sitting behind them."

"Is it possible," thought Edward, "that these can be the two girls who cooked and washed clothes and fed the hens ten years ago in the forest?" As he passed, he looked at Edith and smiled.

"Alice, that's Edward!" she cried, loudly enough to be heard by the King. He too looked up and smiled.

"So those are the sisters of whom you have spoken, Edward," he said. "They must come to my court, and show my French friends how beautiful English women are."

As soon as they could leave the King, Edward and his two friends hurried to the house of Chaloner's aunts. The girls' hearts were filled with joy at seeing their brother again after long years of waiting; they received Chaloner and Grenville, too, as old friends.

"Now, Edward," said Alice, "who do you think was here to-day; the most beautiful woman in London!"

Although Edward knew well whom Alice meant, "Indeed!" he said, "and who is she?"

"Patience Heatherstone," answered Alice with a smile. "She is staying with her father. He has come to London with Humphrey, to see about building Arnwood again. We know all about the trick that

"So those are the sisters of whom you have spoken."

Mr. Heatherstone played. He is ready to give Arnwood back to you."

During the years that had passed, Edward had few chances of finding out whether Patience would wait so long for him. He had written to her, but had received no reply. He thought that his letters had not reached her. This was indeed the reason, for it was then almost impossible for an escaped Royalist to send letters to friends in England, or to receive letters from them. Cromwell's officers were always on the watch to stop all letters that passed between Royalists and their friends. Edward was very doubtful whether Patience would remember the promise that she had made to him when he said good-bye to her. He asked Edith, "Is Patience still unmarried?"

"Yes, indeed," replied Edith. "Although many men have asked her to be their wife, she cares for none of them."

Hope sprang again in Edward's heart. That evening, King Charles held his first Court. Edward stood behind his chair. One by one the gentlemen and ladies of the Court were led up to the King to bow and kiss his hand. Edward was becoming rather tired of the long line of people passing before the King, but it was his duty to stay until the end. Then suddenly he saw Mr. Heatherstone, leading a lady by the hand. It was Patience! Alice had indeed spoken truly when she called her the most beautiful woman in London. Patience bowed to the King, lifted her head again, and looked straight into Edward's eyes. At first she did not seem to know him; the years had made a great difference in the young man who had followed his King to France. Then she smiled, and Edward knew at once that she would keep her promise.

But the King too had seen that smile. With a laugh he turned his head to Edward. "I fear that I shall lose both my bravest officer and the most beautiful lady of my Court," he cried.

A year later the King honoured three officers of his Guard by being present at their marriages. As he gave Patience to Edward, Alice to Chaloner, and Edith to Grenville, he said, "Could there be any finer return for the services you have given to your King?"

There is little more to tell. Humphrey continued to love his work, and Edward gave him a large farm. Some time later he married Clara Ratcliff, who, just before the King's return, had been discovered by an almost forgotten uncle in the West of England. She lived with him until his death, when he left her all his money.

And so we say good-bye to the "Children of the New Forest".

QUESTIONS

1.   1. Where was Colonel Beverley's home?
      2. How many children had he?
      3. What were his children's names?
      1. Why did Colonel Beverley's servants follow him?
      2. Where had Jacob lived all his life?
      3. Where was King Charles's prison?
      1. "It was soon known that ——" What was known?
      2. Where did Jacob stand?
      3. Who was born in the forest?
      1. Why was Jacob surprised?
      2. What could be hidden?
      1. "These old houses are full of ——" What?
      2. What will drive forth any man?

2.   1. Where was Miss Judith sitting?
      2. What did Mrs. Beverley ask her to do?
      3. What had Jacob seen in the forest?
      1. "No enemy of King Charles can ——" What?
      2. How did Miss Judith think the soldiers would treat her? "As ——"
      1. "Jacob knew that ——" What did he know?
      2. What did Jacob tell Edward to do? "Get ——"
      1. What did Edward ask? "Is ——?"
      2. "An old woman remains ——" To do what?
      3. What is an aunt?
      1. Where were the girls playing?
      2. "I must tell you one thing." What did Jacob tell Edward?
      3. Where was Jacob's gun hanging?
      1. When did the children leave Arnwood? "Just before ——"
      2. Whom did Miss Judith tell Jacob to send to her?
      1. Where did the soldiers tie their horses?
      2. Who was sitting at the table?
      3. What could Jacob see?
      1. What was Miss Judith doing?
      2. What did Southwold think?
      3. When did the soldiers set fire to the house? "As soon ——"
      1. Where were the soldiers staying?
      2. "Edward's heart was full of ——" What?
      3. What passed through Edward's mind?

3.   1. What had happened to the house? "It was almost ——"
      2. "They both fell off and ——" What?
      3. What did Benjamin ask one of the soldiers?
      1. "Kill the little foxes; Yes, but ——" What?
      2. Where did Jacob find the children?

1. What did Humphrey and Alice do?
2. Where did Edward stand?
3. "Here are some —— " What?
1. "You could and your sisters must —— " What?
2. "Edward kissed her, and told —— " What did Edward tell Edith?
1. What could Jacob not do every day?
2. Who ate the children's dinner?
1. What did the children prepare?
2. "You seem —— " What did Edward seem?
1. Where did Jacob ride?
2. Where had the King been sent?
1. "You must now wear —— " What?
2. Where did the children run?

4.
1. What did Jacob wonder? "What was —— "
2. What name must the children take?
1. What must Humphrey learn to do?
2. "Little Edith can —— the hens and —— them."
1. What did the children eat at breakfast?
2. "You must be hidden, because —— " Why?
3. Where was the wind?
1. What did one of the deer do?
2. "You put your foot on —— " On what?
1. "Jacob and Edward again went on —— " What?
2. "He tried to rise and run, but —— " What did the deer do?
1. What did they bring to carry the deer home?
2. What did Jacob bring for Edward? and for Humphrey?
3. What did Edward start to do?
1. Why did Jacob and the boys go out?
2. "Sometimes she burnt —— " What?
1. When was Edward sometimes sad?
2. What did Edward wish?

5.
1. What appeared on the trees?
2. "He —— the ground and —— the seeds." What did Humphrey do?
1. What did the plants and trees give them?
2. How long had they been living in the forest? "Exactly —— "
1. "The old man found that —— " What?
2. What tired Jacob?
3. "No one must know that —— " What?
1. "I feel like —— " What did Edward feel like?
2. "The old man is getting very —— and very —— "
3. "I should ask for —— " What would Edward ask?
1. "They would treat you as —— " How would the King's enemies treat Edward?
2. "I can do nothing while —— " What?

6.   1. What was the girl gathering?
      2. Where was the man sitting?
      1. What did the gentleman look at?
      2. "He has some —— which gives us ——"
      1. "We need them to ——" Why did they need the dogs?
      2. "He has taught you to be ——" What?
      1. "I serve ——" What did he serve?
      2. "You will break the law if ——" If what?
      1. Where was the girl standing?
      2. Where did Edward go? "Along a —— to the ——"
      3. Where was the King living?

7.   1. "Then I suppose that ——" What did Oswald suppose?
      2. "It will be difficult for you to ——" What?
      1. What followed Edward?
      2. Where were the King's friends?
      1. "It will be your duty to ——" What was Edward's duty?
      2. What was Jacob's secret?
      3. Why was Oswald delighted?
      1. How many deer did they kill?
      2. Why might Edward lose his way? "The forest ——"
      3. What must Edward climb?
      1. Why could Edward not sleep?
      2. What was the woman trying to do?
      1. What did Edward break?
      2. What did he shout?
      3. What did the neighbours pass to Edward?
      1. What did the voice cry?
      2. Where was the Intendant led?
      1. Where did they lay Patience?
      2. What did Oswald bring from the house?
      1. "I will receive no ——" What?
      2. How did they find Jacob?
      1. What will they find in the wooden box?
      2. Where did Humphrey and his sisters kneel?

8.   1. How long had Jacob been in his grave?
      2. "The King has no ——" What?
      3. "He ordered me not ——" What did the Intendant order?
      1. "—— was raised to guard him." What was raised?
      2. What did Edward know?
      1. "She will never be happy until ——" Until when?
      2. Where did Oswald and Edward go?
      1. "I do not kill —— for ——" What did Edward not do?
      2. Where was the sword hanging?
      1. What was marked on the sword?
      2. What did the gun-maker think was quite fair?
      3. "I would not lose this sword for ——" What?

1. What did they do when they finished their business?
2. Who was the man who spoke to Oswald?
1. "If he sees you in Lymington, ——" What would happen?

9.
1. What did Humphrey ask his brother?
2. What did Edward discover?
1. Where did the brothers go?
2. What did Edward not forget?
1. What was the name of Edward's dog?
2. What blew on Edward's face?
3. "He saw the new King ——" What?
1. How was the stranger dressed?
2. What are no longer allowed in the forest?
3. "My orders are ——" What?
1. "Walk on ——" Where?
2. "I am not so foolish as to ——" What?
1. What did Edward feel?
2. "The forester began to think that ——" What?
1. Who opened the door?
2. "I do not believe that you are ——" What?
3. Why had Mr. Heatherstone quarrelled with the rulers?
1. What did Edward carefully hide?
2. Where had he been taught to read and write?
1. What did Edward discover?
2. Who was Patience's mother?

10.
1. Who was waiting for Edward?
2. "I can take no favours from ——" From whom?
1. When did Edward set out?
2. Who lay asleep on the ground?
1. Where was Corbould standing?
2. Why did no explosion follow?
3. "I was trying to kill ——, not ——" Whom was he trying to kill?
1. What did Corbould shout?
2. What had people taken from the hole?
1. "There was only the light of the ——" What?
2. What did Edward hear?
1. When did Edward reach home?
2. What did Oswald think?
1. "It was difficult to ——" To do what?
2. What happened when the wheels went over a stone?
3. For whom did they send?

11.
1. What did the land give them?
2. What had they made in the open space?
3. What did Edward feel?

1. "The Intendant has the right to ——" What?
2. Why did Mr. Heatherstone go to London?
1. "There will be plenty of ——" What?
2. What was Edward's mind full of?
3. What did Edward do with the sword?
1. "He knew that ——" What?
2. What would guide him?
3. Where did he hide?
1. "Say we are ——" What?
2. What had each man in his hand?
3. Who went to the front door?
4. Where was Ben standing?
1. What did the man near Edward do?
2. What was on the floor?
3. What could Edward see?
4. What came into the man's face?

12.
1. What did Edward put to the man's lips?
2. Where did he lay the boy?
3. "He did not seem to be a ——, ——, or ——" What?
4. How did Edward find the boy?
1. When did Edward wake?
2. "All around was ——" What?
3. What did Holdfast find?
1. What did the brothers decide?
2. What did the boy remember?
3. How long had the boy lived in the house?
1. "I feel ——" How?
2. What was on the floor of the bedroom?
3. "At last they came to ——" What?
4. "Why does she ——" What?
1. What was the girl's name?
2. What did she do when they put her to bed?

13.
1. About what did the Intendant not say a word?
2. What did Edward show the Intendant?
3. Why could not Edward leave the boy in the house? "Other ——"
1. "The dead man is a well-known ——" What?
2. "I will not allow you to speak such words against ——" Whom?
3. "Dig a hole in ——, and put —— and —— into it."
1. Whom did Edward find in the house?
2. "I want to tell you that ——" What?
3. What were the Intendant's real feelings?
1. Why did Mr. Heatherstone join the Roundheads?
2. "I will treat her ——" How?
3. What did Humphrey tell Edward?

1. Where did Clara go?
2. "Of course, he found ——" What?
3. Where did Clara often sit when she was a little child?
1. Why was Clara no longer afraid?
2. Why did the Intendant speak angrily to Edward?
3. "I don't help him much by ——" By doing what?
1. What was in the great box?

14.
1. What did the Intendant send Oswald to say?
2. What did the Intendant think?
1. "I wish to ask ——" What?
2. What did Mr. Heatherstone arrange to do?
1. What did the Intendant need?
2. What did Edward find in the house?
3. What had they placed on the table?
1. "I think your sisters are ——" What?
2. What can Alice do?
3. What did Patience hope?
1. What did Edward think would be very unpleasant?
2. What did Edward decide?

15.
1. What was Oswald glad to hear?
2. How did the Intendant receive Edward?
3. Why did Humphrey smile?
4. What kind of a hat did a Royalist wear?
1. What did Patience and Clara show to Edward?
2. "I am a poor ——" What?
3. "Would I be so friendly with the Intendant if ——" If what?
1. What did Edward do in the morning?
2. What did Edward learn from the keeper?
3. What did they find Alice doing?
1. "He told me that ——" What?
2. What did Edith cry?

16.
1. Where did Humphrey tie his horse?
2. What were the two men doing?
3. How many other men joined them?
1. "They must be ——" Who?
2. What did Humphrey see?
3. What did Humphrey discover?
4. What had the men got in their hands?
1. What came past Humphrey's ear?
2. "He had left the girls at the house —— ——" How?
3. What did Edward promise?
1. Who ran to meet Humphrey?
2. What did Alice help Humphrey to do?
3. What did Humphrey cut in the doors?

1. What did Humphrey know?
2. What held the door closed?
3. Where would the girls be safer?
1. What did the thieves break?
2. What did Humphrey send into the bedroom?
3. "Soon they had pulled —— and —— away from the door."
   What?
1. Whom did they find in Alice's bedroom?
2. What did they do to the prisoners?
3. What did Humphrey take with him?
4. What was in the box?

17.
1. Where did the King land?
2. Who wrote the letters to the Intendant?
3. What would the King's enemies do when they had gained
   what they wanted?
1. Where was Cromwell marching?
2. What happened to the King's army?
3. What did Patience send to the two girls?
4. What did Edward want to do?
1. What was Cromwell doing?
2. What did Clara and Patience promise to do?
3. What did Edward take down from the wall?
4. "You should use ——, not ——" What?
1. What did Edward receive from the Intendant?
2. What woke Edward?
3. "I forgot —— which I meant to give to you." What?
4. "No, read it and think of ——" What?
1. "Soon he was riding ——" What was he riding?
2. What was the name of the Inn?
3. Where did Mr. Langton live?
4. "I will send your letters to ——" To whom?
1. Which was the most important letter?
2. What did Edward tell Samson to do?

18.
1. When did Edward arrive at Barnet?
2. "He walked ——" Where?
3. "For —— I would ——!" What did the man shout?
1. Why did Edward take no notice?
2. What is a highwayman?
3. "In these —— times, we —— have to take in ——" What
   did the innkeeper say?
1. What did Edward do to his pistols?
2. How far did he ride?
3. Why did he stop his horse?
4. What did the third highwayman do?
1. "If you had not been there to ——, I should now be ——"
   What did the rider say?

2. "They made up their minds to ——" What?
3. How old was the stranger?
4. Where did they stop at night?
1. "By your —— I suppose you to be ——" What did the stranger say?
2. What was the name of Chaloner's friends?
1. Where was Chaloner's father killed?
2. "If I did not —— from my ——, I should have ——" What did Chaloner say?
1. What did Edward's father command?
2. What did Edward tell Chaloner?
1. "When you meet the King, you must ——" What must Edward do?
2. Where was Portlake built?
3. What did they learn from the letters?
4. Where was the army that night?

19.
1. When did the letter arrive?
2. What was Edward changed into?
3. Where did the General take them?
4. "I have —— that the son is —— as ——" What did the King say?
1. "I heard that ——" What had the King heard?
2. "He has given orders that ——" What?
3. Where did the army march?
1. Where was Lord Derby taken by surprise?
2. What were the generals quarrelling about?
3. How long did the army stay at Worcester?
4. How far away was Cromwell's army?
1. "They found most of the officers and men —— and ——, but —— to fight."
2. Where did the King ride?
3. Where had Cromwell sent his horsemen?
1. "—— me," said the King. "We must stop this —— fear from ——"
2. "Chaloner at last knew that ——" What?
3. Why did the King ride away alone?

20.
1. "The only danger is ——" What?
2. Where did they ride? "Over ——"
3. How many men were left dead or wounded?
1. Why will they pass through the country safely?
2. When did they come to the inn?
3. "They soon found that ——" What?
4. Where did they sleep?
1. Where was Humphrey?
2. What did he do at first?
3. Where did Edward see Oswald?

1. Why was Mr. Heatherstone surprised?
2. What must Edward arrange to do?
3. "Her —— soon changed to ——"

21.
1. What did Edward learn?
2. "They must —— here, and work like ——" What must the girls do?
3. What did Edward know?
1. Where was Humphrey working?
2. What did Edward show the soldiers?
3. Why did the soldiers go to the sea-coast?
1. What was granted to the Intendant?
2. What did the Intendant doubt?
3. What did Benjamin give to Mr. Heatherstone?
1. "Now I shall never be ——" What?
2. "Some day I hope that ——" What?
3. What will the Government never know?
1. What could Edward offer Patience?
2. "If the King ——, I must —— with him in ——" What did Edward say?
3. What was Patience doing?

22.
1. What did Edward show Alice?
2. Who were Edith's friends, too?
3. What did Humphrey buy in Lymington?
4. What did they sail in?
1. Where did the girls live?
2. What did Edward become?
3. What did the French make King Charles do?
1. What did the ladies wave?
2. What did the two girls do in the forest?
3. What must the girls show the King's French friends?
4. Who was the most beautiful woman in London?
1. Why did Edward receive no reply to his letters?
2. What did King Charles do that evening?
3. What was Edward's duty?
4. What did Edward know when Patience smiled?
1. What did Edward give to Humphrey?
2. Whom did Humphrey marry?

Pronunciation of the chief names of persons and places

THE pronunciation given is the system used in The International Phonetic Alphabet.

Armitage	ˈaamitidʒ
Arnwood	ˈaanwud
Barnet	ˈbaanit
Benjamin	ˈbendʒəmin
Bolton	ˈboultən
Captain Marryat	ˈkæptin ˈmæriət
Chaloner	ˈtʃælənə
Clara	ˈkleərə
Colonel Beverley	ˈkəənəl ˈbevəli
Corbould	ˈkɔɔbould
Cromwell	krɔmwəl
Cunningham	ˈkʌniŋhəm
(Lord) Derby	ˈdaabi
Grenville	ˈgrenvil
Heatherstone	ˈheðəstoun
Holland	ˈhɔlənd
Humphrey	ˈhʌmfri
Hurst	həəst
(The) Intendant	inˈtendənt
Isle of Wight	ail əv wait
Jacob (Armitage)	ˈdʒeikəb
James Southwold	ˈdʒeimz ˈsauθwould
Judith Villiers	ˈdʒuudiθ ˈviliəz
Lambert	ˈlæmbət
Langton	ˈlæŋtən
Lymington	ˈlimiŋtən
Middleton	ˈmidltən
Naseby	ˈneizbi
Oswald Partridge	ˈɔzwəld ˈpaatridʒ
Patience (Heather-stone)	ˈpeiʃəns
Portlake	ˈpɔɔtleik
Ratcliff	ˈrætklif
Samson	ˈsæmsən
Spain	spein
Warrington	ˈwɔriŋtən
Wigan	ˈwigən
Worcester	ˈwustə
York	jɔɔk